PILL
CITY

Kevin Deutsch is an award-winning criminal justice writer for *Newsday* and previously worked on the staff of the *New York Daily News*, the *Miami Herald* and the *Palm Beach Post*. He is the author of *The Triangle: A Year on the Ground with New York's Bloods and Crips*. Kevin teaches journalism at Queens College and lives in New York City.

ALSO BY KEVIN DEUTSCH

The Triangle:
A Year on the Ground with
New York's Bloods and Crips

P LL

C TY

HOW TWO TEENAGERS FOILED
THE FEDS AND BUILT A DRUG EMPIRE

KEVIN DEUTSCH

PAN BOOKS

First published 2017 by St Martin's Press

First published in the UK in paperback 2017 by Pan Books
an imprint of Pan Macmillan
20 New Wharf Road, London N1 9RR
Associated companies throughout the world
www.panmacmillan.com

ISBN 978-1-5098-4330-5

1 3 5 7 9 8 6 4 2

A CIP catalogue record for this book is available from the British Library.

Printed and bound by CPI Group (UK) Ltd, Croydon, CR0 4YY

Visit **www.panmacmillan.com** to read more about all our books
and to buy them. You will also find features, author interviews and
news of any author events, and you can sign up for e-newsletters
so that you're always first to hear about our new releases.

For Laura

Not everything that is faced can be changed, but nothing can be changed until it is faced.

—James Baldwin

Contents

Author's Note

The following is a work of nonfiction. It is based on interviews with more than 300 opiate dealers, drug addicts, treatment experts, law enforcement officials, gang members, and others. Additionally, it draws on thousands of documents, including law enforcement records, autopsy reports, death certificates, and several sales databases provided to the author by Pill City's co-founders.

In order to disguise the identities of interviewees, most of their names have been changed. For that same reason, certain locations, physical descriptions, and other identifying details have been altered or obscured. In addition to gang members and addicts, I spoke at length with a number of social workers, physicians, and police officials as well as federal agents involved in the investigation of street gangs and looted drugs. Many of these men and women requested their names be changed, since revealing their identities would have compromised their work, and likely jeopardized their jobs. Most of my interviews with officials were conducted after the events described in these pages. For the purpose of narrative cohesion, I've interwoven their accounts of the investigation into all five sections of the book.

As for methodology, I conducted most of my interviews with gang members and opiate addicts on the fly, spending many hours with them in their homes, vehicles, and on drug corners. With regard to dialogue, all conversations and quotes appear verbatim as they were recounted to me; the result of hundreds of hours of interviews and on-the-ground reporting in Baltimore, South Florida, Kansas City, St. Louis, Chicago, New Orleans, Connecticut, and New York City. About 50 percent of the events chronicled in this book are based on interviews. The rest, I witnessed firsthand. I've used interior monologues or referenced a subject's thoughts only in cases where I interviewed them extensively about their thinking at a particular moment.

For purposes of clarity, the term "opiates" is used throughout this narrative to describe both heroin and prescription painkillers.

* * *

This book tells the story of one of the most profitable illicit opiate dealing schemes in American history, and the tech-savvy teenagers who helped pull it off. The earliest of their syndicate's crimes—brazen, well-planned heists of approximately 50 pharmacies, drug corners, and stash spots—occurred during a 25-hour period on Monday, April 27, and Tuesday, April 28, in Baltimore, Maryland, as rioters burned and looted properties across the city in response to the death of Freddie Gray.

The unrest has cost city government alone about $20 million. But the riot's human toll—the number of lives lost and families destroyed due to pilfered drugs—remains incalculable. Approximately $100 million worth of narcotics stolen in Baltimore flooded America's streets in the months after the riots, creating scores of new addicts. Bloody turf battles were waged between heavily armed gangs battling over those drugs, conflicts that left at least 91 young men, women, and children dead across the country in 2015 and at least 187 others injured. Entire families succumbed to deadly overdoses, creating a generation of parentless kids dubbed "Generation Pill" by social service workers. And a pair of impoverished tech geniuses from Baltimore's West Side transformed scores of inner-city drug markets, their actions making them heroes in the eyes of some but the cruelest kind of killers to others.

At the height of the teens' success, their "franchises" were trafficking more than a quarter billion dollars in opiates. This book tells the story of the damage these gangsters inflicted, from their first pharmacy break-in to the latest bullet fired in "Pill City." It also chronicles the bloodiest organized crime conflict America has seen since the days of Al Capone and Murder Incorporated—this one fought not by bootleggers but by inner-city-dwelling, opiate-slinging gangsters.

Last, this work explores the impact of opiates on heavily black, low-income census tracts across the country, places where addicts and their families continue to suffer in silence, deprived of both resources and attention.

In these pages, I have tried to give them voice.

—Kevin Deutsch, Baltimore, March 2016

Glossary of Terms

BGF—the Black Guerrilla Family gang

Dark Web—an unindexed part of the Internet accessible only through an encrypted browser

dope, raw—heroin

dope sick—sickness caused by withdrawal from opiates

enforcer—a gang member who commits homicides and other acts of violence to protect his gang's interests

field marshal—a high-ranking member of BGF; usually oversees a team of enforcers

Frankenstein—heroin cut with fentanyl

hot shot—a deadly dose of heroin

Percs—Percocet

Pill City—a Baltimore-based drug syndicate founded in April 2015

re-up—to obtain a new supply of drugs from one's supplier

rig—a syringe

riot pills—pills stolen during the April 2015 riots

Roxys—Roxicodone

spike—an unused needle

twin—a communal syringe shared by multiple addicts

vacant—an abandoned property, usually a rowhome, in Baltimore City

Vikes—Vicodin

Key Players

The Dealers

James "Brick" Feeney—cofounder of Pill City

Willie "Wax" Harris—cofounder of Pill City

Lamonta "Lyric" Johnson—BGF set leader

Desmond "Damage" Vickers—BGF field marshal

Dante "Slim" Robinson—BGF enforcer/dealer, Iraq War veteran

Christopher "Train" Lockwood—BGF enforcer/dealer

Jimmy Masters—leader of the Masters Organization, a Baltimore-based drug syndicate

Ezekiel "Zeke" Masters—Jimmy's younger brother, responsible for the family's operations in Kansas City, Missouri

Stephan "Stacks" Masters—Jimmy's son, drug dealer

Andrew "Blackrock" Masters—Jimmy's son, responsible for the family's operations in South Florida

Kenny "Mondo" Mack—Jimmy's nephew and security chief

Lionel "Dome" Simmons—BGF enforcer

Raheem Wallace—computer hacker, high-ranking member of the Youngstown Boys drug syndicate

The Customers

Keisha Jones—opiate addict, mother of a six-year-old boy

Terry Augman—opiate addict, pregnant with her first child

Derek Curry—opiate addict, former professional jazz guitarist

Otis Washington—opiate addict, former sanitation worker

The Investigators

Frank Calvacca—Narcotics detective, Chicago Police Department

Jamal Grayson—Narcotics detective, Baltimore Police Department

Jeffrey Madigan—Gang detective, Newark Police Department

Mike Malinowski—Sergeant, Baltimore Police Department

Kirstin Marques—Special agent, Drug Enforcement Administration

PART I

THE RISING
PLAGUE

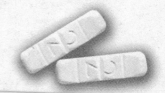

"An Uber of Drug Dealing"

There's enough narcotics on the streets of Baltimore to keep it intoxicated for a year. That amount of drugs has thrown off the balance on the streets.

—BALTIMORE POLICE COMMISSIONER ANTHONY BATTS

April 28, 2015, West Baltimore

James "Brick" Feeney and Willie "Wax" Harris are standing on the corner of Mosher and North Mount Streets, pistols tucked into their waistbands, toothpicks dangling from their lips. To their right, Fred's Discount Pharmacy is engulfed in orange-red flames, its marquee shrouded in a cloud of gray smoke. To their left, five members of the Black Guerrilla Family—Baltimore's biggest, most powerful gang—are bashing in the head of a dealer who'd just encroached on Brick and Wax's territory. It's a seemingly minor offense but one that will get dozens of young men killed here in the coming weeks.

"Boy had it coming," says Brick, loading a fresh clip into his Glock G26. "He knew the rules."

"Too bad, though," replies Wax, slipping a black ski mask over his face, then switching the safety off his own pistol, a

P229 Sig Sauer. "Shit's going to get hot with all these bodies dropping."

Twenty-four hours ago, this pair of high school honor students, both 18, might have seemed the unlikeliest of drug kingpins—Brick, with his concave chest and pigeon-toed walk, and Wax, with his wire-frame glasses, Payless sneakers, and potbelly. Best friends since age 10, the precocious pair had rarely missed a day of school, much less masterminded a major narcotics conspiracy. But that was before Freddie Gray died on April 19 from spinal cord injuries suffered in the back of a police van; before the riots set off by his death turned Brick and Wax into bona fide underworld giants in control of a drug empire soon to be worth tens of millions of dollars—"an Uber of drug dealing," as Brick calls it—that will transform the way illicit opiates are sold in wide swaths of urban America and help fuel a wave of addiction and homicide in some of the nation's poorest enclaves.

"After today, with all the pills we got and all the homies we got soldiering for us, we ain't got to worry about money ever again, no matter how hot shit gets," Brick says as he and Wax enter Fred's Discount. "All the mess we've been through . . . it's over."

When they come sprinting out of the burning store 10 minutes later, covered in ash, each is dragging a Hefty trash bag filled with bottles of prescription Percocet, OxyContin, Vicodin, Roxicodone, Opana, and Zohydro—powerful painkillers that sell for up to $100 each, or about $1 per milligram, on America's drug corners. The heist is just the latest in a string of brazen thefts executed by the teens and their BGF cohorts over the past 25 hours, crimes that have targeted approximately 50 pharmacies and illicit drug stashes throughout Baltimore while police were busy responding to arson and looting elsewhere in the city. In total, the newly minted drug lords and their associates have pilfered approximately $100 million worth of prescription opiates and heroin in a little over a day—a feat unprecedented in the annals of American crime.

"Kind of pretty, ain't they?" says Wax, opening one of the trash bags to reveal a rainbow-like assortment of pink, blue, white, orange, and yellow prescription pills: oxycodone, oxymorphone, hydrocodone, and hydromorphone of every formulation and dosage, each tablet worth roughly its weight in gold.

"The money we get for them going to be even prettier," Brick says.

The friends had fantasized about a moment like this since the day they met, reading Iceberg Slim's autobiography *Pimp* on the stoop of a local heroin den while their mothers got high inside. Later, in middle and high school, they'd bonded over a mutual love of technology and literature, devouring crime fiction and westerns—paperbacks like *The Godfather* and *Lonesome Dove*—by the stack. The books inspired them to contemplate their own capers—not the harebrained drug deals that got so many of their peers killed or imprisoned, but something high tech and sophisticated: a data-driven, criminal enterprise unlike anything Baltimore had ever seen.

And finally, tonight's riots had given them the chance.

"We going to do this right," Wax says. "Like we always talked about."

The duo's approach to opiate dealing will be ruthless and innovative—a blend, Wax says, of "Wall Street–style profit maximization, and Silicon Valley–style disruption." With Brick's programming, hacking, and financial expertise—he's been studying the stock listings in the *Wall Street Journal* and *Baltimore Sun* since he was 11 years old and making mock online trades since he was 12—coupled with Wax's genius for software development, coding, and all things digital, the computer virtuosos figure they can achieve something no drug-dealing duo has in the long, sordid history of Baltimore's drug markets: staying power.

"Soon we'll be running this whole damned city, steady putting out product like those Mexican cartels do," Brick says, loading the bags of stolen pills into his 1998 Honda Civic, a rusted, sad-looking heap of steel he'd purchased six months earlier with money from his after-school math tutoring job. Before they get into the car, Brick fingers the Glock in his waistband, his lips curled in a mischievous grin.

"Yo, you want to?" he says.

Wax thinks on it for a moment, scanning the street for cops. But there are none in sight, just the teens and their BGF accomplices, still whaling on the trespassing dealer outside Fred's Discount. Senior among these gangsters is Brick's second cousin, Desmond "Damage" Vickers, 24, who'd helped forge the partnership between BGF and the enterprising teens.

"Come on, yo," Brick prods his friend. "Now or never."

"Fuck it, why not?" says Wax, pulling out his Sig.

On the count of three they aim their guns at the sky—just like the bandits in those westerns they'd grown up reading—and empty their clips toward the stars. The staccato rhythm of gunfire sounds almost festive to them, an ear-splitting, celebratory coda to their daylong binge of drug looting.

"Let's go!" Brick says, jumping into his Civic after the last shot's been fired. He tries the key in the ignition five or six times before the cranberry-colored four-door finally starts, its engine sputtering as exhaust fumes flood the street behind them.

"With all this money we about to get, maybe you can get a

new whip," Wax says. "'Cause honestly, this Honda's whack as hell."

"Yeah, yeah, and you can replace them goofy-ass glasses," Brick says, relishing the back-and-forth with his old friend.

"Man, my glasses are fly!"

The teens laugh as they drive off, knowing there will be plenty of cash at their disposal after tonight: money to buy cars, computers, clothes, sex, and anything else they can dream up. They've even given a name to their bourgeoning syndicate: Pill City.

"Whatever happens," says Wax, bumping fists with Brick, "we do this thing together."

"Most def," Brick says, hitting the accelerator. "Like always."

The crimes committed by Brick, Wax, and their underworld accomplices tonight are just the beginning—a precursor to the plague of addiction and overdose that will ravage America's poorest, most racially isolated inner-city neighborhoods in the months to come. It's a plague fueled not just by the profit-hungry pharmaceutical companies and pill-peddling doctors we hear so much about, but by hundreds of thousands of opiates stolen in Baltimore while no one was watching.

"You've got to blame the doctors and the drug makers, no doubt, but on a street level, it's the dealers who are driving a lot of this mess right now," says Jamal Grayson, a Baltimore narcotics detective who is part of a team of local, state, and federal law enforcement officials tasked with capturing Baltimore's drugstore looters. "When they got their hands on those pills [during the riots], it was like stealing the nuclear codes. In Baltimore and a lot of places like it, those drugs are blowing up whole neighborhoods."

Whereas America's "first wave" of postmillennium opiate abuse helped kill nearly half a million drug users between 2000 and 2014—whites, blacks, Hispanics, and members of every other minority group—this postriot "second wave" is disproportionately affecting African Americans, according to public records and interviews with dozens of addicts, doctors, dealers, treatment experts, and law enforcement officials. Even before the Baltimore drug lootings, opiate abuse among blacks was on the rise. The rate of heroin overdose deaths soared 213 percent among African Americans between 2000 and 2014, the largest increase ever in that category, according to the Centers for Disease Control and Prevention. In 2015 and 2016, amid the epidemic's second wave, things have gotten worse: While blacks represent about 13 percent of the U.S. population, they now account for approximately half of all overdoses caused by illegally purchased opiates, records suggest. In blighted urban areas, it's nearly impossible to find a block untouched by the epidemic.

"Things are looking grimmer out here every day, to tell you the truth," says Brayonna Oakley, 43, of East Baltimore, whose 19-year-old old son, Adonde, fatally overdosed on looted oxycodone he brought from a BGF dealer in June 2015. "So many African Americans are dying from this stuff, but no one wants to address the impact of it [the opiate epidemic] in black neighborhoods. Until we do, people like my son will keep dying."

The deeper one digs into the data, the worse things look.

Painkillers and heroin killed nearly 30,000 Americans in 2014, about 19,000 from pills and 10,600 from heroin. Nationally, nearly 130 Americans die each day from drug overdoses, more than a quarter of whom identify as African American. Hundreds of disenfranchised blacks narrowly survive opiate overdose each week, revived by the life-saving, opiate overdose antidote naloxone. Many others die without ever receiving the drug, a result of naloxone shortages in their communities.

But in spite of a mounting death toll in neighborhoods of color, the black and brown aspect of the opiate epidemic receives scant attention from the press, politicians, and law enforcement, experts say, flying under the radar even as the national media breathlessly covers the same scourge in white suburbs.

"Because the demographic of people affected are more white, more middle class, these are parents who are empowered," Michael Botticelli, director of the White House Office of National Drug Control Policy, said of the epidemic's impact on suburban and rural families. "They know how to call a legislator, they know how to get angry with their insurance company, they know how to advocate. They have been so instrumental in changing the conversation."

But for those living in poorer, blacker neighborhoods ravaged by opiate abuse, the opposite scenario is playing out. In these disadvantaged communities, few residents can get the attention of lawmakers, health department officials, or journalists. Most receive substandard addiction treatment, experts say, or none at all. And while the communities described by Botticelli continue to be politically "empowered" amid America's opiate epidemic, scores of lower-income blacks are suffering in silence, deprived of much-needed government resources and media attention.

"We've got black people dying of heroin and pills on a large scale but . . . nobody's really talking about it, because the epidemic in white communities is getting all of the notice," says Dr. Morris Copeland, an addiction treatment specialist in Newark, New Jersey, whose patients are predominantly black.

"It's like there's only enough air in the room for us as a society to focus one aspect of the epidemic, the white aspect. But in communities of color, people are hurting just as badly."

Indeed, 53 of the 100 census tracts with the highest opiate overdose rates in 2014 had majority-black populations, records show. In the nation's five most populous cities—New York, Los Angeles, Chicago, Houston, and Philadelphia—the rate of African Americans who die with heroin or opiate painkillers in their system is higher, per capita, than that of whites or Hispanics. Yet there's little public discourse about the toll opiates are taking in these struggling communities. Proof of this disparity lies in the amount of press coverage on the topic: Since 2013, more than 22,000 news stories published in American media outlets have made mention of "white," "suburban," or "rural" addicts battling opiate addiction. Meanwhile, *fewer than 20* such stories have focused on black opiate addicts living—and dying—in poverty-stricken cities during that same period.

"Now all of a sudden heroin has made its way out into the white suburbs, and the attention that is being given to it I applaud, but it is attention that quite frankly should have been given to this epidemic a long, long time ago," Baltimore's current police commissioner, Kevin Davis, said of the epidemic's racial dynamic.

Scores of men and women fighting to curb opiate abuse in America's inner cities—cops, doctors, and addiction counselors alike—say looted drugs are helping to drive up overdose rates, harming black families in some cities on a scale not seen since the crack epidemic of the 1980s.

"It's as devastating a scourge as we've seen in terms of drugs being abused in impoverished African American communities, and it traces back, in many cases, to the pharmacy lootings," says Grayson. "We're talking about the equivalent, in terms of an organized drug score, of the Brinks Truck Robbery or the Lufthansa Heist, really notorious crimes. The difference is, the goods stolen this time were very addictive, very powerful drugs . . . that are killing people in places already dealing with high rates of poverty and violence."

The number of drugs looted in Baltimore, officials say, is staggering.

At least 314,920 prescription pills were reported stolen from 32 Baltimore businesses—31 retail pharmacies and one medical office inside a methadone clinic—during the riots, according to the Drug Enforcement Administration's official tally. Of those pills, 133,798 (42 percent) were opiates. As of this writing, not a single pill has been recovered, the agency says.

Troubling as these numbers are, they tell only half of the story. Equally concerning to drug investigators are the estimated 300,000 to 400,000 doses of *illicit* opiates BGF members stole from rival dealers during the unrest, drugs that include black-market pain pills, methadone bottles, fentanyl, lab-manufactured opiates, and millions of dollars' worth of heroin, according to multiple law enforcement officials at the federal, state, and local levels as well as drug dealers and gang members involved in the robberies. The drugstore lootings alone "represent the largest transfer of prescription drugs from private hands to the hands of drug dealers in this country—ever," says DEA Special Agent Kirstin Marques, who, like Grayson, is tasked with capturing pharmacy looters. About a third of Baltimore's pharmacies were looted during the riots. No criminal organization—not the mafia, the Bloods, the Crips, or any transnational drug cartel—has ever plundered so many prescription narcotics in so short a time span. Nor has any robbery spree triggered so much violence so quickly.

"There's enough narcotics on the streets of Baltimore to keep it intoxicated for a year," Anthony Batts, Baltimore's police commissioner during the riots, said of looted drugs on June 3, 2015. "That amount of drugs has thrown off the balance on the streets."

Within weeks of Freddie Gray's death, stolen opiates from Baltimore found their way to impoverished neighborhoods in Detroit, Memphis, Milwaukee, Philadelphia, Cincinnati, Atlanta, and Indianapolis, fueling a surge in gun violence. Later, pilfered narcotics arrived in some of the poorest sections of South Florida, St. Louis, Kansas City, Camden, Newark, Bridgeport, Memphis, Cleveland, and dozens of other impoverished, majority-black communities, all without fanfare.

Within these blighted areas, homicide totals quickly spiked, as did both fatal and nonfatal opiate overdoses. Today, legions of slurring, glassy-eyed addicts continue to overwhelm drug rehabilitation facilities in these areas, while hospitals struggle to handle an influx of overdosing and withdrawing patients. In Maryland alone, recorded overdose deaths from drugs and alcohol rose 21 percent in 2015, to 1,259, while fatal overdoses from fentanyl spiked 83 percent, to 340. "The numbers in relation to drugs stolen during Baltimore's unrest are indeed troubling," said Christopher Garrett, a spokesman for Maryland's health department. As drug addicts pay a heavy price, so, too, do dealers. At least 118* men, women, and children have been killed nationwide in homicides connected to drugs looted from Baltimore, plus an additional 227 injured. Overall, at least 416 people believed connected to the

---

* Death totals in this section are drawn from the author's analysis of autopsy reports, public health data, police records, court filings, and interviews with dealers, narcotics investigators, drug treatment experts, and relatives of deceased addicts.

illicit opiate trade in America were killed in homicides during 2015 alone, with at least 448 others hurt in nonfatal shootings, stabbings, assaults, and other criminal acts, records show. The carnage continued in 2016, with more than 450 people killed in violence connected to the illicit opiate trade.

In many impoverished parts of the country, a new kind of underworld battle is being waged, conflicts so deadly and hard to suppress that they've been given their own monikers.

"We call them the Opiate Wars, or Pill Wars, because they're really their own style of conflict," says Jeffrey Madigan, a gang detective with the Newark Police Department in New Jersey, which has investigated at least four homicides linked to Pill City. "There's a ferociousness in these market-share battles in these neighborhoods that we hadn't necessarily seen in the cocaine wars or in disputes between marijuana or meth dealers. This conflict is bloodier, more organized, more driven by technology. And much of the violence we're seeing is connected to those drugs stolen during the riots."

Grayson says the scheme to steal and sell those looted opiates, both on the streets and through the Dark Web, is "probably the most heartless thing I've seen done, premeditated, by a drug gang."

He adds: "For two 18-year-old kids to run a business like this, to help put together this plan . . . it's genius, from a criminal's perspective. But it's also just about the most horrible thing you can do to places that are already suffering from poverty and violence."

"Getting Paid"

It's like somebody opened up the spigot and drugs started pouring out. This here's heaven for an addict.

—Derek Curry

April 29, 2015, Greenmount Avenue, West Baltimore

"Got that body bag," a BGF dealer shouts.

"Got that killa," yells a second.

"Y'all need to get with this raw," a third slinger bellows.

In response, a steady stream of customers stops to inquire about each stash of looted opiates—morphine, Zohydro, heroin, and more—before forking over fistfuls of cash. Then, drugs in hand, they hustle off to swallow, snort, or inject their illicit drugs. It's just after 11 p.m. on a Wednesday, and BGF's on pace to make more money tonight than it has during the past 30 days. *Combined.*

"I can barely keep up they coming so fast," says the first dealer, as customers stuff singles and fives into his palms.

When a female addict tries to pay him in quarters, the

slinger smacks her in the face with an open palm, ordering her to come back only when she has "cash money."

"Damn, fiends be out in force tonight, for real," he says.

"Long as they paying, it ain't no thing," one of his colleagues says.

None of the gangsters or addicts gathered here can recall so many high-powered opiates being sold this cheaply, or with such little interest from police. The riots, they know, have flooded Baltimore's drug markets with a staggering amount of heroin and pills, much of it being sold at bargain basement prices by BGF. As for the absence of cops, many are so angry about the unrest and criticism of police that followed Freddie Gray's death, they've decided to "back off, let the dealers do what they do," as one Baltimore police sergeant put it.

"I ain't never seen anything like this," Derek Curry, a long-time opiate addict, says after buying three bags of heroin and some Zohydro capsules from BGF. All around him, Greenmount is packed with jittery pill and dope buyers, some of them everyday users, others there to cop for the first time, enticed by BGF's discount rates. "It's like somebody opened up the spigot and drugs started pouring out," he adds. "This here's heaven for an addict."

Curry would know. A former professional jazz guitarist, the one-eyed addict's been scoring pills, heroin, and the occasional bag of cocaine on these streets since the 1990s. But he's never experienced anything like tonight's "free-for-all," he says.

"I bought some dope from a boy on the corner two blocks from here back in the day, shot up, and never looked back," says Curry, 53, who'd made his living playing music for almost three decades, recording a number of albums before his opiate addiction "became a full-time job." Around the time he gave up performing, Curry lost his wife, Cassie, to a fatal OxyContin overdose, holding her in his arms as the drugs slowed, then stopped, her breathing.

"I don't like to talk about it, or remember it, even," says Curry, squeezing through the window of a vacant rowhome, one of a handful of places he likes to boil down and inject his narcotics. "The drugs, they help me forget."

While Curry readies a fresh rig, the Greenmount drug market keeps humming, each deal happening under the watchful eyes of BGF's four most senior members: Lamonta "Lyric" Johnson, Desmond "Damage" Vickers, Dante "Slim" Robinson, and Chris "Train" Lockwood. The gangsters are sitting in Train's GMC Yukon, eyeing the trio of younger dealers in the street to ensure they're not "messing around instead of moving product," says Train, who manages BGF's dealing crews in the greater Baltimore area.

"Niggas doing good out there so far, coming correct," Train says, toking on a tightly rolled blunt in the driver's seat. The SUV's interior is thick with marijuana smoke, Ghostface Killah's *Twelve Reasons to Die* blasting from the speakers, as the gangsters conduct what they call "quality control."

"It's like that show *Undercover Boss*," says Train. "Except if our people fuck up, they might catch a bullet instead of unemployment."

The other gangsters crack up at the line, dizzyingly high on the weed they've been smoking, thrilled to see their pilfered opiates reaching so many customers. Throughout Baltimore's poorest neighborhoods tonight, BGF corner crews like the one on Greenmount are moving heroin and riot pills at a breakneck pace, Train says, while the gang's fleet of delivery men are bringing looted drugs right to customers' doors, guided by encrypted messaging and dispatch software of Brick and Wax's design.

Already Baltimore's largest, most powerful street gang, BGF's partnership with the teenage software engineers has brought its earning power to "a whole new level," says Damage, who, in addition to being Brick's cousin, is the set's field marshal and second in command. He'd orchestrated the deal between the gangsters and the teenage tech wizards, ensuring that looted drugs will reach other BGF sets, or franchises, in 28 major U.S. cities in the coming weeks.

"I feel like we going to be getting money like this every *night* from now on," says Damage. "Only question is, how hard are Jimmy and his people going to come at us after they tool up [prepare to retaliate]?"

Damage is referring to Jimmy Masters, 68, one of Baltimore's leading heroin, marijuana, and pill traffickers, a gangster as famous for his elegant dress as for his violent temper. His family-operated crime syndicate, the Masters Organization, has long controlled the flow of illicit opiates and weed into many of Baltimore's poorest, most violent neighborhoods—or had, anyway, before BGF raided Jimmy's drug stashes and killed or wounded a number of his associates during the riots.

"Jimmy and his people ain't got no fight left, not after what we done to them," says Lyric, his gold-capped teeth sparkling under the Yukon's dome light.

The brawny, bald 27-year-old—who's committed at least five murders during his gangland career—was recently thrust into the gang's top spot following the murder of his predecessor, Darryl "Red" Whitmore, Damage's closest friend. Since Red's death, the relationship between Lyric and Damage has been fraught, each distrusting the other's leadership abilities. The riots have enriched the gang but also served to deepen the rift between its leaders.

"We got them running like bitches right now," Lyric says of Jimmy's men, "not like when Red was running shit."

"You right," says Slim, 26, BGF's third in command, passing Lyric a second, newly lit blunt. "Damage just tripping, worrying over nothing as usual."

Damage, lounging in the front passenger seat, clicks his tongue at the slight. Now that Red's gone, Lyric and Slim seem to be going against his advice more frequently, calling his combat strategies into question on a daily basis. As field marshal, he's officially tasked with plotting BGF's drive-by shootings, walk-up killings, and other crimes targeting rival crews. But Damage thinks that Slim, who'd served two tours in Iraq before returning to gang life, is making a brazen play to take over as field marshal, the Army veteran regarding himself a superior tactician.

Yet even Damage can't quibble with the quality of Slim's work.

Over the past few nights, the ex-soldier has decimated Jimmy's ranks in ways few thought possible, roughing up a number of his corner dealers, murdering or seriously injuring several of his lieutenants, and—with the help of other BGF members—robbing nearly three quarters of Jimmy's heroin and pill stashes during the riots.

"Jimmy's crew, they finished," Slim says. "That shit ain't in doubt."

Damage doesn't like the way Slim's running his mouth, but for now, he decides to put up with it. After all, the partnership Damage negotiated between BGF, Brick, and Wax is already earning BGF sets around the country tens of thousands of dollars, a deal more valuable than any murder Slim might commit.

"Keep on talking that shit, nigga," Damage says, eyeing Slim in the rearview mirror. "And I'mma make sure we keep getting paid."

"The United States of Addiction"

We're not like other hustlers. Not even close.

—Brick

Several miles east of Greenmount, BGF's teenage business partners are unpacking a trove of new computer gear inside their "office"—a dilapidated vacant on a poorly lit, lightly traveled stretch of road. The home is nearly uninhabitable, plagued by a leaky roof, plus-size roaches, and an army of rats. Yet the hardware Brick and Wax are setting up inside is top of the line: lightning-fast, Linux-loaded computers, private servers, high-powered laptops, big-screen monitors, scores of data storage devices, and, in the middle of it all, a pair of propped-up plywood boards–*cum*–computer desks. All the electronics are brand new, ordered with loans from BGF. And more arrive every day.

"I thought we couldn't do worse than the projects," Wax says, surveying their grim surroundings, "until we got here."

"This our home away from home now," says Brick. "Better get used to it."

Whatever its faults, both teens are excited to have a larger space to work in, along with powerful equipment to keep Pill City's operations humming. Before now, they'd been doing all their programming from the Gilmor Homes, where the boys live with Wax's mom, Brenda Harris. The encrypted messaging/drug delivery program they'd created there has already proven stunningly effective, allowing dealers in multiple cities to communicate without fear of digital surveillance. By year's end, their software will have been used by at least 44 BGF sets across the country, gangsters relying on it to receive encrypted drug orders, make doorstop deliveries, and organize re-ups in at least 110 economically depressed neighborhoods.

"Things are going good out there, no doubt," Brick says as he and Wax settle in behind their desks. "But in here, with all the new gear we got, we're going to make them even better. We're going to do what they do out in Cali: disrupt, dismantle, change the game."

Brick's a cocky, smooth-talking kid who can parrot the language of Silicon Valley one minute and that of urban drug corners the next. His conversations are peppered with financial lingo, too; a result, he says, of his regularly perusing the websites of *Forbes*, the *Wall Street Journal*, and *Bloomberg*, along with various hip-hop-influenced entrepreneurial ones.

"We all about them dollars, just like them white boys in Silicon Valley," he says. "We do what they do, but we do it in these streets."

"Hopefully, we going to make the same kind of dough as them, too," his partner says.

Wax is quieter, less cocky, but he's just as smart. Peers in the underground programming community say he's one of the top young software engineers in the country. Like Brick, Wax can hack even the most well-protected network after just a few days—sometimes hours—of probing for weak spots.

"I ain't going to lie," Brick says. "We're both good at what we do."

And they're not alone.

Pill City employs more than half a dozen security associates—hackers and programmers who belong to the hacktivist group Anonymous. Over the past two years, Brick and Wax have assisted the group with a number of hacking operations, some targeting white supremacist websites, others going after ISIS-linked accounts on social media. As a result, they'd had little trouble recruiting Anonymous members as counter-hackers, experts who help keep Pill City's networks safe from malicious hacks and government surveillance. Within a few weeks of the riots, these associates configured all Pill City computers with emergency passwords meant to wipe their hard drives clean should authorities ever seize them.

"They're helping us out, 24/7 . . . as much for the money as they are the politics," Brick says. "They're angry about racist police . . . they're angry about what the cops did to Freddie [Gray]."

"So it makes sense that they'd want work with us," adds Wax.

Listening to the boys discuss their business, it's easy to forget they're operating a sprawling, destructive, illegal drug network rather than a legitimate startup. Even the handwritten notes taped to their walls contain Silicon Valley–like mottos like "Make Ideas Happen" and "Move Fast and Break Things"—reminders, they say, of the "disruptive" philosophy they've applied to the drug game.

"We," Brick says as the boys set to work on a new page of code, "are the new disruptors."

To understand how they reached this moment—safely ensconced in their Baltimore office, with their Dark Web drug marketplace thriving and hundreds of dealers using their software to blanket blighted neighborhoods with drugs—it helps to set aside the tropes of traditional, inner-city slinging: the petty beefs, the sagging jeans, the obsession with disrespect. Investigators say none of these characteristics applies to Brick and Wax—at least not yet—and that's what makes them so scary to federal agents and local detectives, none of whom has yet gotten a bead on the teens' true identities or whereabouts. Most of this reporter's interviews with the teens have been conducted via encrypted email or messaging, a reflection of the lengths they'll go to maintain their anonymity.

"It's a different approach from what we're used to seeing from [dealers] in urban areas, the level of caution," says Marques, the DEA agent. "As far as the paradigm for corner dealing goes, these guys seem to have thrown it out the window."

Whereas traditional drug gangs typically are led by undereducated teens and 20-somethings "prone to overreaction," Marques says, Pill City's leaders appear to be "reflective and calculating." And where their underworld predecessors often behaved recklessly, Pill City's founders have "shown a preference for operating in the shadows," using encryption to mask their lawlessness.

"They don't behave like inner-city drug dealers, not in the traditional sense," says Frank Calvacca, a Chicago narcotics detective. "They behave like a couple of young guys who moved to Silicon Valley to try and strike it rich."

Perhaps that's because Brick and Wax don't see themselves

as criminals but rather as self-described "underground hackers and entrepreneurs." Before founding Pill City, they say, they'd learned a great deal about traditional corner dealing, having spent their childhoods in the care of heroin-addicted mothers, even copping drugs for the women on occasion. Then they built a system to overtake the corner-dealing model that had kept their mothers high, letting software do the heavy lifting once required of drug kingpins. In rejecting that "corner-focused paradigm," Marques says, the teens have also rejected the calculus of traditional dealing—the grim math that allows one out of perhaps 100 gangsters to avoid the graveyard or jailhouse and, as Brick puts it, "earn their way out the ghetto."

"We're not like other hustlers," Wax says of the syndicate's low-tech predecessors. "Not even close."

Ask them how they became friends, and both boys speak of the abuse, violence, addiction, and mental illness that permeated their youths, all of it leading up to an icy, windswept morning in December 2007, in the thick of what Brick calls "the most messed-up days of my life."

"Dear God," Brick whispered into the silence of his bedroom that morning. "Please keep Arthur away. And please make the heat come on. If you do, I promise I won't never sin. Amen."

According to Brick, it was just after 9 a.m., and he was shivering beneath his Baltimore Ravens covers. The heat was broken again, but Arthur Kane and his live-in girlfriend, Brick's mom, Renata Feeney, didn't seem to mind. All they cared about these days was getting high and staying that way.

"James, you awake?" the gruff voice in the hallway said, followed by the sound of James's bedroom door creaking open.

Both sounds made the 10-year-old sick with dread, for they meant that Arthur would soon be lying beside him, the overpowering smell of his aftershave filling the room. James—still months away from earning his nickname—feigned sleep, even pretended to snore, but it didn't matter.

"I always know when you faking," Arthur said, easing himself under the sheets.

James kept a running count of the times Arthur sexually assaulted him—that day's attack made 23—but he still had no idea how to stop the abuse. During the first incident, in March 2006, James screamed, punched, and kicked Arthur hard as he could, only to be beaten unconscious. Afterward, he'd prayed for two hours straight, begging for "divine intervention," something he'd heard about in church back when his mom used to take him every Sunday.

Still, nothing changed, leading James to wonder whether "anybody up there was listening."

Like many citizens of West Baltimore, the Feeneys were Southern Baptists, a God-fearing family who'd settled in Baltimore during the Great Migration and produced several generations of factory workers, home builders, and clergymen. They were working-class strivers, people who believed in the value of education and steady work. But when the crack epidemic came to Baltimore, they suffered as badly as any other family.

Renata Feeney's father got caught dealing rocks and went to prison, where he died of a heart attack on the floor of his cell. Her mother remarried and moved to Missouri, leaving Renata and her sisters in the care of an uncle, himself a crack addict. The uncle ended up dead as the result of a drug dispute; other relatives met similar fates, dying from homicides, suicides, overdoses, and AIDS. Those who survived fled the city fast as they could, but not Renata.

By the late 1990s, she was the only Feeney still living in

Baltimore. Nine years after Brick was born, she became a heroin addict herself and moved in with Arthur Kane.

"That was the worst time for us," her son recalls.

After the first few assaults, James chose to endure Arthur's abuse silently, believing his resistance only made things worse. Instead of fighting, he'd pray or daydream, often thinking of the books he'd read, stories of swaggering heroes and bandits from the old West, or cops and robbers—anything to take his mind off the reality of his situation. Afterward, Arthur would return to the living room, where Renata would either be nodding off in front of the TV or slamming home another dose of heroin.

Arthur, 33 at the time, supported both his and Renata's drug habits with landscaping work. And while Renata despised him—he abused her and her son verbally, physically, and sexually—she stayed with him more than two years, mostly because he bought her "as much heroin as she could shoot," her friends say. Arthur also paid for what Renata called her "head pills"—pricey medication she took for the bipolar disorder she'd battled since her teens. On some level, James understood his mother's predicament—he, too, would battle bipolar disorder in his teenage years, experiencing exhilarating highs and debilitating lows. But he could never understand why Renata ignored his screams the first time Arthur slid beneath the covers with him—or the second, or the third.

"Mom!" he'd bellowed loud as he could, only to hear her raise the volume on the TV.

On that December morning in 2007, though, James's fortunes began to change. His mother had just injected the last of their heroin, and Arthur, emerging from the boy's room to find the supply exhausted, grew furious. He landed a hard right hook to Renata's left eye and ordered her to go out and buy more drugs. She did as she was told, yelling for James to "hurry up and get dressed" so she could take him to McDonald's on their way back. Renata was not immune to her son's suffering, Brick would later say; she'd simply deprioritized it to sustain her addiction and pill regimen.

"I got to make a stop, but we'll get you breakfast right after, OK?" Renata said as they walked to the neighborhood shooting gallery, a one-stop shop where addicts from across West Baltimore purchased and injected heroin.

James said nothing, moving slowly through the soft early morning light, his body still sore from the assault. Along the way, they passed the church they'd once attended, mother and son worshiping there together for years. Gazing at the spire set against the gray Baltimore sky, James recalled how good it had felt to sit in the church pews; how safe. But as soon as they'd moved in with Arthur, he'd ordered them to stop attending services, calling religion "a bunch of bullshit." Then came the rapes, the beatings, the verbal abuse. James tried to put prayer out of his mind as they passed the church, deciding it wasn't doing him any good.

"Almost there," Renata said, rubbing James's shoulders to try to keep him warm.

When mother and son reached the shooting gallery, they found the usual crowd of fiending addicts, switchblade-carrying hustlers, and scantily clad prostitutes fresh from their overnight rounds. But one face stood out from the rest. Sitting on the backdoor stoop was a chubby, bespectacled boy no older than James himself, doing something James had never seen done outside a school classroom.

He was reading a book.

"Go play with him," Renata said, knowing her son had no greater passion than reading. "I'll be right out."

James was a shy kid at the time, plagued by low self-esteem, ashamed of his victimization by Arthur. He had no friends to speak of, though he desperately wanted to make some. Seeing the pudgy boy on the stoop, he did a quick calculation. His mother would be gone at least 30 minutes, since the line to buy heroin already snaked out the door, and Renata would probably shoot up inside, too—just a little dope to dull the pain around her swelling eye. With so much time to kill, James decided to gather up his nerve, walk over to the boy, and say hello.

"What's up, man?" James said softly. "What you reading?"

Willie Harris looked up from the book, adjusting his glasses to get a better look at this stranger. He wore bleach-spotted khakis, a paint-spattered Terps cap, and a too-big flannel shirt that belonged to Arthur Kane—not much cleaner than Willie's own outfit, consisting of a moth-chomped, Chef Boyardee–stained fleece and a crusty, too-tight pair of Levi's.

"Ain't reading nothing," Willie said, unsure if this sunken-chested kid was really interested in his paperback or only making fun of him. "Just waiting for my moms."

Willie had just finished chapter two of *Pimp: The Story of My Life*, the autobiography of Iceberg Slim. Someone had forgotten it at the Laundromat where Brenda Harris did their wash every other week, and Willie scooped it up. A 10-year-old boy had no business reading a tale so full of sex, drugs, and violence, he knew, but that's precisely what spurred him to take it home—and what made reading it so exciting.

Willie couldn't understand half of what the author had written, but he knew Iceberg Slim was the kind of man you didn't mess with, and that losing himself in the pimp's story had helped him forget his own assorted fears: that his mother would die of an overdose inside the shooting gallery; that she'd be beaten bloody, yet again, by one of her johns; or that she'd simply give up on Willie one day, walk out of their apartment in the Gilmor Homes and never return.

"Yeah, I'm waiting for my mom, too," James said. "She gets me books sometimes, if she remembers. But most of the time I go to the library on my own."

Readers were a rare sight in their neighborhood, Willie knew, with the ratio of discarded syringes to books being easily 10 to 1. If this kid really did like reading, Willie decided, maybe they *could* be friends.

"It's called *Pimp*," Willie said, flipping the book around to flash its silver and purple cover. "It's by a guy named Iceberg Slim."

"Man, I've been trying to find that book everywhere!" said James, who'd tried to check *Pimp* out from the public library a few weeks earlier, only to be stopped by the head librarian, who told him the book was "for grown-ups only."

"You like it so far?" James asked.

Like it so far? The truth was, Willie *loved* it. He'd been dying to delve into the book all week, but his mother had been dope sick in recent days, constantly summoning him to help her in and out of the bathroom. Caring for Brenda left Willie little time for reading or homework. But this morning, she'd finally scraped enough money together to score, dragging Willie with her to the shooting gallery.

"Yeah, it's real good," Willie said. "I can't understand a lot of it. But I'm *positive* this man doesn't play."

James was impressed. He'd never met anyone his age who read books for fun, much less ones about pimps and gangsters. He himself devoured novels in his room at night, the exciting tales helping him cope with real-life villains like Arthur Kane. Realizing there was someone else like him in West Baltimore— a boy who loved reading, whose Mom had the same debilitating addiction—made James feel, for the first time, like he wasn't alone.

"If it's cool with you," James said, gesturing toward the book, "can I borrow it when you're done?"

"Most def," said Willie. "We could even read some now if you want."

Seconds later they were seated side by side on the stoop, ignoring the addicts and prostitutes parading past, reading along at the same, frenzied pace. By the time their mothers stumbled out the shooting gallery, arms lined with fresh track marks, James and Willie were a quarter of the way through the tome.

"See you tomorrow?" James said as Renata yanked him up from the stoop, anxious to buy her son breakfast and get home with Arthur's drugs.

"Most def," said Willie, reaching out just in time to bump fists with his new best friend.

If books formed the foundation of Brick and Wax's friendship, the teens say, it was technology that kept it going. Both were enamored with computers even before they'd met, wowed by the sleek, futuristic design of the new iPhone and MacBooks as well as the stunning speeds at which they processed information. Librarians they knew let them use digital devices of all kinds, and the friends quickly mastered the state-of-the-art gadgets. By their 12th birthdays, there was no online task Brick and Wax couldn't perform: Coding, software design, and rudimentary hacking all had a place in their repertoires. And what they couldn't glean on their own, they learned from more experienced tech geeks online.

"It came natural to us," Wax says of hacking and programming. "And we were hungry to learn."

Their high-tech education came at a unique historical moment, for computing in America had never been more accessible nor cutting-edge technology more ubiquitous. Breathtaking new products were coming out of Silicon Valley every day, new tech millionaires seemingly being minted by the hour. On TV news shows and the *Wall Street Journal*'s business pages, Brick learned about the hottest tech companies: Apple. Facebook. Google. To him and Wax, these weren't just businesses—they were the embodiment of everything they wanted out of life: prestige, power, and, most of all, money.

The drug dealers in Gilmor worked to attain those prizes with guns and knives, but Brick and Wax believed they could capture them with passion, intelligence, and technology. And if laws had to be broken along the way, that was OK, too, for they'd already adopted a motto by which they would live—an axiom to guide them in their hunt for life's biggest prizes:

Behind every great fortune there is a crime.

It was a Balzac line that served as the epigraph for Mario Puzo's *Godfather*—a novel Brick and Wax would each read at least half a dozen times during their high school career.

"Those words weren't just words to us," Brick says of the quote. "They were a worldview. So yeah, we admired the tech companies who'd made their money legally, but we knew even legitimate companies have to do improper things to get where they are, that they get in the gutter and do dirty shit on occasion. Behind every great fortune's a crime, right? So we weren't necessarily opposed to doing illegal things like selling drugs, doing dirt, whatever had to be done to make money."

For two boys born to heroin addicts, living in one of the most forlorn ghettos in America, computers offered the dual comforts of logic and control, things lacking in their everyday lives. On the streets, Wax couldn't control the amount of heroin his mother injected. At the keyboard, though, he was continuously in command, using clear, verifiable code to create logical functions and "make sense of the world." For a cerebral, chubby kid growing up in the projects, the ability to build software and hack websites was the ultimate tool of empowerment—a ticket to a world where, just as in the books he loved, Wax could be the hero of his own, thrilling story.

"This is the hottest thing we've ever done," Wax told Brick after the duo wrote their first piece of working software together on their own computers in 2009, a program that tracked the boys' grades and homework assignments. It was one of the few pieces of software the friends, then 12, would produce that *didn't* involve illegal activities. And it paved the way for their more lucrative collaboration down the road.

"Shoot, this is just the beginning," Brick said of the software.

Just as they'd been for Wax, books were Brick's intellectual escape hatch. But in computers, he found something he loved even more: a tool that allowed him to *create* new realities, not just imagine them. Only when programming could he forget about his mother's addiction and block out the memories of Arthur Kane's abuse.

"Online, you can be anyone—hustler, hacker, killer," he told Wax.

Their work with computers, while certainly a labor of love, served a practical purpose, too. Brick and Wax knew they'd need a special set of skills to strike it rich—an area of expertise that could land them in a plush apartment downtown or a fancy house like the one like Brick's drug-dealing cousin, Damage, owned out in Baltimore County. The alternative, they knew, was to stay in Gilmor and suffer the fates of so many classmates and neighbors: drug addiction, prison time, death by bullet or blade.

In contrast to the projects, no place seemed more glimmering with possibility to the boys than Silicon Valley. There, in sleek office buildings dotting the Santa Clara Valley, tech titans hardly older than Brick and Wax were building fortunes out of coding languages the boys had already mastered— C, C++, Java, Python, HTML, Prolog, and others.

"If those white boys can do it," the friends wondered, "why can't we?"

In high school, they breezed through their classes with straight As and a handful of Bs, bored by "dumbed-down" coursework in an underfunded, failing school, Wax says.

When junior year ended, they had two options: apply for college, or seek their fortunes as tech entrepreneurs. The choice seemed like a no-brainer.

"Why should we go to school for four years when we're ready to build a business now . . . to make money today instead of down the road?" Brick recalls thinking. "The idea of college . . . we understood what it could mean, but we felt like we didn't have that kind of time. We didn't know if we'd even be *alive* to go to college. Anybody can catch a stray [bullet] around here, or roll up to the corner at the wrong time and get killed."

Such fatalism is common among children living in violent, drug-plagued neighborhoods, and it affected Brick and Wax as much as any of their classmates. Their apartment was located on a block that, per capita, ranked fifth poorest in the city and the third likeliest on which to be killed by a gunfire. Given their surroundings and the scope of their talents, no one could blame them for wanting to make as much money as quickly as they could.

"We're from the hood, from a broken place, no matter how you dress it up," Wax says.

"We wanted to make enough money to lead a better life, whatever it took," says Brick.

So instead of applying for college and student loans, they worked tirelessly on software development, programming, and hacking, biding their time until the right opportunity came along.

"And when Freddie got arrested," Brick says, "everything just came together."

"The Purge"

It may sound like a story arc from a TV series, but it is real life in Baltimore.

—U.S. Attorney Rod Rosenstein

West Baltimore

Before he became a symbol of police violence and racism—before Brick, Wax, and BGF used his death as a business opportunity—Freddie Gray was "just a poor black man living in West Baltimore, trying to make ends meet," his family says.

Known to friends as "Pepper," Gray, 25, was a gregarious, "happy-go-lucky guy" who made his living selling small bags of marijuana and dope in and around the Gilmor Homes, those who knew him say. He was as tough as any slinger on the corner, according to friends and family, yet aspired to "do something more with his life."

"Freddie always had a smile for you, and a word of encouragement," says his cousin, Tim Thomas, 19. "He could have done anything if he'd been born someplace where there was opportunity. He was always singing funny songs, making jokes. I think the [police] wanted to crush that spirit in him."

Gray told friends he wanted to earn his GED, attend community college, and "get a job involving electronics," perhaps working as an electrician or air-conditioning repairman. But to the cops who knew Freddie—officers who'd watched him sling product day after day, despite numerous drug arrests—he seemed little more than "a small-time hustler," says one police official. Police took him into custody April 12, 2015, after he ran from them—he was later found to be carrying a small pocket knife—then tossed him, his legs shackled and wrists handcuffed, in back of a police transport van. On the ensuing ride, Gray suffered massive trauma to his spinal cord and neck—injuries that later killed him. Descriptions of his treatment, when they hit the news, sparked outraged across Baltimore.

"Five-O has got to go!" a group of protestors chanted at the corner of North Avenue and Mount Street on April 15, a few feet from where Gray was arrested. When a police squad car rolled past, one demonstrator removed a pink balloon from his backpack and hurled it at the vehicle, sending what appeared to be feces splattering across its windshield.

"Fuck y'all pigs," the balloon hurler shouted. "We ain't going to let y'all rest."

Watching coverage of Gray's arrest on WBAL Channel 11, Brick and Wax say they were equally furious. They lived five buildings away from Gray in the Gilmor Homes and considered him a friend.

"I loved Freddie," says Wax. "He always stopped and chilled with us when he passed our building. He didn't deserve none of what happened."

The fact that, in Brick's words, Gray had been "kidnapped off the street by a gang of cops" was no surprise to the young programmers, given that young black men were "constantly getting picked up over bullshit out here.

"But we were also kind of *glad* people were so angry," Brick says. "Because chaos always presents an opportunity in business, if you know where to look."

The teens were drug-dealing novices at the time of Gray's arrest but, thanks to their mothers and Damge, were hardly strangers to the game.

"We looked up to Damage and them, most def," Wax says. "But we wanted to start a business that let us use our [computer] skills to make money."

Ever since that day on the shooting gallery stoop, Brick and Wax had dreamed of getting rich, just like Iceberg Slim. But what started as a fantasy now actually seemed within reach. Few kids their age were more skilled when it came to software development, coding, and hacking. And, even at 17, the duo "knew [they] were qualified" to work in Silicon Valley, says Wax.

"But we knew the statistics, too," he adds. "They didn't look too promising."

Indeed, just 2 percent of Google's and Yahoo's workforces were black at the time, and just 7 percent of Apple's. With those odds, success in the legitimate tech community seemed remote, the boys thought. So instead of looking west, they turned their attention to a local project—one with considerably more risk than a traditional tech startup.

Inspired by Dark Web drug markets like Silk Road, Agora, White Rabbit Anonymous Marketplace, and Outlaw Market, Brick and Wax had begun sketching the contours of their own illegal drug website—one that would rely on encryption, data analysis, and technology rather than traditional street sales.

After school each day, they'd study these "invisible cartels," Dark Web marketplaces that are impossible to trace to their administrators—and customers—when properly used. As far as the teens were concerned, these weren't just lucrative criminal enterprises; they were legitimate tech startups, as sophisticated as anything those "white boys" in Silicon Valley had put forth.

"It's brilliant," Wax said when he first scrolled through Silk Road's drug menu. "I think we can do the same thing."

The boys knew plenty about encryption—the use of secret keys or passwords to keep data hidden from prying eyes—but neither had had a real need for it before the riots. Seeing how the anonymity tool was being used to peddle drugs, though, "made a light bulb go on" for the teens, Wax says. Encryption, they realized, was helping to create a new class of criminal—digital gangsters who oversaw drug operations without fear of arrest; young men who'd built multimillion-dollar fortunes with nothing but keystrokes and a little courage.

"We wanted a piece of that industry," Wax recalls. "It was just a question of how."

The boys were still working on their plan for a Dark Web marketplace when Gray was arrested. As tensions in Baltimore rose, some of Gray's friends vowed to wage a "war on pigs" or "blow up downtown" if he died, while others called on the Baltimore police commissioner, Anthony Batts, to resign. Two days after Gray's arrest, doctors at Shock Trauma Hospital performed a double surgery on his spine, hoping to save his life.

"All that time he was in the hospital, people kept getting angrier and angrier," Brick recalls. "You could see the violence coming."

On April 18, as Gray lay comatose in his hospital bed, protests erupted outside the Western District police station. Activists from the Black Lives Matter movement called for criminal indictments of the officers involved in Gray's arrest,* while more radical protestors called for "rioting and revenge."

The next morning, April 19, Gray died of his injuries.

"People going to tear up the West Side," Brick predicted that afternoon while scrolling through his Twitter feed. Almost every tweet he saw called for attacks on cops and other acts of violence. On Wax's Facebook page, friends were calling the anticipated unrest "the Purge," a reference to the 2013 movie in which all laws are suspended for 12 hours, allowing criminals to act with impunity.

"This," Brick said of the anticipated unrest, "is what we've been waiting for."

The time was ripe, both boys agreed, for them to turn their dream of building an encrypted drug market into reality. Authorities were so busy dealing with protestors and the press, Brick said, they'd have little interest in the Internet activity of two project kids.

"If not now," Wax remembers thinking the day of Gray's death, "when?"

"If those boys in Cali can do it, so can we," said Brick. "The drugstores . . . that's how we can get product to [start the business]. I bet Damage and his people would help us out, too."

If looting drugstores seems like a perilous way to secure inventory, the teens thought it preferable to the alternative: another year spent in a failing, violence-plagued school; another year of watching helplessly as Brenda Harris worked the streets and flirted with death; another year, as Wax put it, "of feeling dead without being dead." The partners believed with

---

* A Justice Department investigation later found that the police department routinely violated the civil rights of African Americans.

certainty that they could make themselves rich with their programming skills. And selling drugs, with the help of encryption, suddenly seemed like their best bet.

"Around here, you could be breathing one minute, smiling and happy, then gone," says Brick. "Just look at what happened to Freddie. That's why you take your opportunities when you get them. Especially in the game."

The teens knew drug dealing in Baltimore was low tech and archaic, relying in 2015 on the same supplier-to-middleman-to-dealer model it has used since the 1960s. They knew, too, that the encrypted online drug markets they admired catered almost exclusively to tech-savvy whites, charging exorbitant prices that most impoverished users couldn't afford. That led the boys to ask themselves: What if they geared their encrypted drug network solely toward inner-city users, promising fast, high-quality service to communities of color? What if they facilitated the delivery of drugs right to addicts' doors, aided by the single most important drug-dealing tool in history: the encrypted iPhone? What if, along the way, they dragged urban drug dealing into the twenty-first century and built a Silicon Valley–sized fortune in the process?

"We can do actually do this," Wax said. "We can hack the corners."

On April 19, they put the next phase of their plan into motion, working day and night to create a new kind of platform for urban drug dealing. Sucking down Red Bulls while listening to Earl Sweatshirt, Kanye West, Scarface, and Lil Wayne, the boys went on a software coding blitz, working round the clock with only short breaks for naps and trips to the corner carry-out for snacks, mostly Doritos and Mountain Dew.

In the end, the program they built blended the mapping and dispatch features of Uber's ride-hailing app with the secrecy of encrypted drug markets like Silk Road, a combination meant to leave law enforcement befuddled, customers satisfied, and competitors overwhelmed. The boys dubbed their software "Harm City," a dark take on Baltimore's nickname, and tweaked it till it operated without a hitch. They would later change the program's name to Pill City, the same title they'd adopt for their syndicate, and go live with a separate, Dark Web marketplace— one accessible only through Tor, the encrypted browser.

"Shit is *right*," Brick said after the first round of software tests. "All we need now is something to sell."

When Damage got home that night, Brick and Wax were waiting outside his house, ready with their "investor pitch," Wax recalls. They explained to him that Baltimore's drugstores would be vulnerable during the Purge so many on social media were predicting. Then they showed him the software they'd developed.

"Ain't nobody going to be guarding those pharmacies if shit gets crazy," Brick told his cousin. "It's the ideal situation for us, now that we got the software ready to go."

"We're going to need help, though," said Wax. "A lot of it."

Damage weighed the pros and cons of the plan. Though he'd recently been promoted within BGF, he remained locked in a power struggle with his new boss, Lyric, as well as Slim, the Iraq War veteran, for control of the gang's "combat operations." Ushering the gang into a partnership like the one Brick and Wax proposed could boost his waning influence, he knew, and make them all a lot of money.

"It's risky as hell," Damage said, "but I definitely want in."

Damage said he viewed the anticipated unrest as a "once-in-a-lifetime chance" and that he would gladly enlist BGF to loot pharmacies, so long as profits were distributed equitably. In addition, BGF would target drug corners and stash houses belonging to one of Baltimore's biggest drug syndicates, the Masters Organization, since the gangs were already locked in a long-running conflict that had recently led to the death of BGF's former leader, Red Whitmore.

"We got 150 soldiers ready to help y'all, since our interests align," Damage said after clearing the idea with Lyric. Their gang consisted of between 130 and 150 members and associates. "All we need now is for shit to pop off."

The next day, Damage brought Lyric to meet with Brick and Wax outside an abandoned waterfront building. The young men were a study in opposites: Lyric and Damage decked out in baggy designer jeans and brand-new Under Armour sportswear; Brick and Wax with their discount-rack dress clothes straight from the Target on Tioga Parkway. When the teens opened their mouths, though, Lyric realized they weren't your average bookworms.

"They started talking about algorithms, data, programming, all the things they were going to do to make our business more efficient," Lyric said. Then they showed Lyric the software they'd been working on. "It looked like Uber, but it was built for [dealers] to get product to customers. It had this messaging feature . . . that kept everything encrypted."

"I was amazed," Lyric added. "We didn't use that kind of technology at the time."

Lyric asked whether the software would work on smartphones outside of Baltimore. After all, BGF had sets or affiliates in at least 31 other cities, all of them involved in various drug-dealing schemes.

"Absolutely," Brick said. "It can be used anywhere in the country."

That was all Lyric and Damage had to hear. The next day, they called up some of America's most powerful BGF set leaders and proposed a multistate partnership—a syndicate that would use Brick and Wax's software to traffic opiates in poor, drug-plagued neighborhoods across the country. Over the course of four days, several dozen BGF sets hashed out profit-sharing agreements with Lyric. They would act as franchises of Pill City, using the teens' encrypted software to receive and organize deliveries but otherwise running their operations as they saw fit. As part of the agreement, Brick, Wax, and Baltimore's BGF set would get a percentage of their earnings.

"The deal benefited everyone," Damage says. "After we hashed that shit out, we started making lists of which pharmacies we thought would be the easiest to hit. And we waited."

While the partners plotted their historic drug heists, protests over Gray's death grew larger—and louder—by the day. On April 24, Police Commissioner Batts acknowledged errors by his department, telling reporters that Freddie Gray "was not buckled in the transportation wagon as he should have been . . . we know our police employees failed to get him medical attention in a timely manner multiple times."

The mea culpa, meant to ease tensions in the city, had little effect. On April 25, demonstrators vandalized a handful of businesses and vehicles in West Baltimore, promising further unrest if police weren't held accountable. The next day, Gray's twin sister, Fredericka, stood beside Mayor Stephanie Rawlings-Blake at a press conference, urging calm.

"Can y'all please, please stop the violence?" Fredericka said, making a plea for peace that echoed Rodney King's 23 years earlier. "Freddie Gray would not want this."

But the entreaty failed, just as it had in L.A. On Monday, April 27, the day of Gray's funeral, riots erupted across West Baltimore and downtown. Roaming groups looted or damaged around 400 businesses, set fire to over 150 structures and vehicles, and attacked cops in the street, leaving about 130 police personnel injured. More than 200 people were arrested during the unrest, including Donta Betts, 20, who would later plead guilty to charges he helped loot a burning CVS pharmacy and built a "destructive device" out of toilet paper and propane tanks to block cops' path to the store.

"I figured I did all this because that was my period of time to go wild on the police," Betts allegedly told authorities. U.S. Attorney Rod Rosenstein said of Betts's crimes: "It may sound like a story arc from a TV series. But it is real life in Baltimore."

In response to the rioting and looting, Maryland's governor, Larry Hogan, summoned the National Guard to Baltimore, and Rawlings-Blake announced a weeklong curfew beginning the night of April 28.

That gave BGF—with Brick and Wax's help—more than enough time to execute their plan. Lyric and Damage dispatched looting teams across the city, each consisting of 10 to 12 gang members and their associates, some male, some female.* As lawlessness spread, the teams plundered drugs from pharmacies as well as from stash houses and drug corners controlled by the Masters Organization, while Brick and Wax—drawing on their electronics expertise—burglarized drugstores with more advanced security systems. In between drug heists, the teens posted incendiary messages about police on social media, hoping to keep the unrest going "as long as possible," Brick says.

By the time the riots were over on April 29, the bourgeoning syndicate had stockpiled a massive collection of heroin and prescription opiates, everything from OxyContin and methadone to fentanyl and morphine. Pills. Patches. Liquids. If a

---

* Dozens of looters unconnected to BGF also stole property during the riots.

pharmaceutical company or illicit drug lab made it, Pill City had it in abundance.

"I don't even know if we can sell all this," Wax said of the gigantic pile of narcotics stored in the syndicate's main stash house in early May.

"This is the United States of Addiction, man," said Brick. "We'll *definitely* sell all this."

"Playing from Behind"

We believe that in some instances gang members specifically targeted the pharmacies for the Schedule II drugs, that being OxyContin, oxycodone, Vicodin and Percocet.

—GARY TUGGLE, ASSISTANT SPECIAL AGENT IN CHARGE,
DEA BALTIMORE OFFICE

May 1, 2015, West Baltimore

Detective Jamal Grayson is icing down his face, still trying to ease the swelling that started when a National Bohemian beer bottle caught him square in the jaw during the riots.

"Thirteen years [on the force], I've never seen that much airmail," says Grayson, using a slang term for projectiles hurled at police. "It was complete chaos."

The veteran narcotics investigator knew Freddie Gray's death spelled trouble. He just didn't think it would be quite so destructive: torched buildings, burned-out vehicles, Grayson and his fellow cops getting clobbered with all kinds of debris. Throughout the riots, he'd stayed put in Baltimore's Penn-North neighborhood, the epicenter of the unrest, trying to talk sense into "pissed-off looters," he says.

"They were so mad, they didn't want to hear it, especially from a black cop," Grayson adds, driving through Sandtown-

Winchester a few days after the unrest, one hand on the steering wheel, the other holding an icepack against his jaw.

"They thought I was being a hypocrite," he adds. "But as a black man, I understand how the riots looked to a lot of people in this country, people who don't necessarily identify with the lives of poor people of color. That's why I was trying to limit the stupidity I was seeing, to keep [Baltimore] from looking bad.

"And this," he says, gesturing toward his puffed-up jaw, "is what I got for my trouble."

A sinewy six foot three, Grayson tends to command any room he's in, even ones filled with the toughest of cops and criminals. Nicknamed "the Beast" due to his powerful physique and tireless—some say even self-destructive—work ethic, he's among the most respected drug investigators in the Baltimore/DC region, having been recognized with just about every award the police department has to offer. Over the past decade, Grayson's been shot at by dealers, bitten by their pit bulls, and struck by a fleeing drug mule's Cadillac. He's tracked down meth cookhouses by scent alone and taken millions of dollars' worth of narcotics off the streets.

And yet, once upon a time, the 37-year-old father of two nearly ended up on the wrong side of the law.

"A lot of bad guys probably wish I did," he says. "I came pretty close."

Grayson grew up on what he calls a "very tough, very poor" street in Druid Hill—a Northwest Baltimore neighborhood that, at the time, was ruled by some of the city's fiercest drug dealers, several of whom offered Grayson work on the corners. Dozens of his friends and relatives were employed by those slingers and made "piles of money" before being wounded, killed, or imprisoned, the detective says.

Grayson was just about ready to join their ranks—envious of their fat wallets, flashy jewelry, and expensive cars—when he witnessed a lowly corner boy, a friend of his named Ronnie "Cush" Spear, get half his head blown off in a drive-by shooting. The sight of Cush lying dead on the pavement so enraged Grayson, he decided to join the police academy instead of a gang.

"I knew the people who did that to Ronnie were dealers who didn't value life, and their callousness . . . enraged me," he says. "I assumed the cops were the good guys."

It wasn't long before the rookie officer experienced racism on the force, everything from taunts about his hair, which he wore in an afro, to mockery of his Muslim upbringing. He worked to reform the department from within, pushing for the hiring of minorities and fighting for better pay. On the streets, he treated African American suspects "decently and fairly," he says, earning respect in neighborhoods where few white cops ventured.

"There were, and are, some knucklehead cops, cops who don't use their heads enough and who don't necessarily empathize with young black men," Grayson says. "I wanted to help change things in our department, which I hope I did, even if we're still enduring many of the same problems we did back then."

These days, Grayson arrests slingers working the same corners he roamed in his youth, locking up guys whose fathers, grandfathers, and uncles he once attended school with. For that reason, his work "is painful a lot of the time, because it allows me to see what's become of these families. The game swallowed almost all of them up."

To Grayson, the "game" of drug dealing isn't just a destructive force in Baltimore; it's a "very powerful, very deadly poison affecting all of Black America," since heroin, pills, cocaine, and marijuana all double as "commodities young African American children and men kill and die for" in droves across the country.

"I consider it my job to stop that destruction, at least in Baltimore," he says. "Even if not everybody in this department takes the job as seriously as I do."

Pronouncements like these have prompted a number of Grayson's colleagues to call him self-righteous, egotistical, even a zealot. He's been known to go long stretches without sleep when working a big case, operating under the belief that, as one colleague dismissively puts it, "he's going to single-handedly win the war on drugs." The detective admits he has a tendency to "go overboard" on his cases, a habit that led his ex-wife—the mother of his two sons—to divorce him in 2012.

"I spent too much time on the job, and my marriage suffered for it," says Grayson, whose boys, Nate and Charles, live with their mother, Lisa, in Southern California. He hasn't seen either child in three years, a gap he attributes to workaholism, along with Lisa's recent marriage to a Los Angeles attorney. "I piss people off sometimes, my ex, my colleagues . . . I know that. But at the end of the day, I outwork everyone."

Indeed, even Grayson's harshest critics acknowledge he's the ideal investigator for the drug-looting probe, a sprawling case involving dozens of gang-affiliated offenders.

"We believe that in some instances, gang members specifically targeted the pharmacies for the Schedule II drugs, that being OxyContin, oxycodone, Vicodin, and Percocet," Gary Tuggle, the assistant special agent in charge of the DEA's Baltimore office, said after the lootings.

Already, Grayson's hearing about those stolen opiates

making their way to blighted parts of Newark, Chicago, Memphis, and other inner-city slums.

They're already killing people, too.

"A half hour ago, we had our first reported overdose" from looted drugs, Grayson says. "Guy in his early 30s, from Penn North. Dead in a motel, needle in his arm, cooked up some oxy and put it in a vein."

On his way home, Grayson is notified of another overdose thought linked to stolen pills. The next morning, he's alerted to two more, including a heroin poisoning possibly linked to a batch BGF stole from the Masters Organization during the riots.

"There's no precedent for a case like this, not really," says the detective. "You've got dozens of pharmacies looted, a lot of very powerful product on the streets. I consider this the most difficult case of my career."

And it will worsen in ways Grayson can't yet imagine.

Two and a half miles from Grayson's home, Patricia "Patti" Sinclair, 39, is sweeping up shattered glass in her father's pharmacy, trying to keep from crying. Fred's Discount Pharmacy is in shambles, ravaged by rioters who'd toppled shelves, set fire to merchandise, and stolen thousands of high-priced prescription drugs. Patti wishes she could confront the looters—"shame them" for their cowardice, she says. But all the anger in the world won't bring back the old Fred's, she knows, not any more than her tears would.

"We'll be OK, Dad," she tells her father, Fred Sinclair, 71, who's squatting over a pile of spilled pills in the corner of the store, cataloging what's left of his drug inventory. "Everything can be replaced."

The father and daughter had tried to assess the damage

here earlier in the week, but were scared away by crews of roving drug dealers—members of the Black Guerrilla Family—who'd been posted up outside their pharmacy like an "occupying force," Patti says. On the sidewalk near the door, a streak of dried blood indicates the spot where the gangsters had savagely beaten a rival dealer.

"What they did out there was bad enough, but I'm afraid what they did in here's going to cost a fortune to fix," Fred tells his daughter. "Problem is, money ain't coming our way no time soon."

The insurance policy on the pharmacy fully covers most every imaginable calamity, Fred explains, from floods and hurricanes to earthquakes and lightning strikes. What it *doesn't* cover fully is damage caused by rioting of the kind Baltimore's just experienced.

"All these years I paid the insurance company, it was a waste," the gray-haired pharmacist says, gesturing at the wreckage around them. "I don't think we can recover without a big payout."

Patti is about to tell her dad he's wrong, that they'll get through this together, just as they had her mother's death a year earlier, when she hears a crackling sound behind her, the crunch of dress shoes on shattered glass. She turns to find a tall, well-dressed black man entering the pharmacy. He winces at the sight of the toppled merchandise, shaking his head.

"I'm sorry this happened," Grayson says, introducing himself to the father and daughter. "It's absolutely awful."

The detective's been visiting looted pharmacies all week but had purposely avoided Fred's until now. The place is so close to his heart, he says, he hadn't wanted to see it in such disarray.

"I know this store like the back of my hand, used to come

in here when I was a kid," he says. Then, smiling at Patti: "I probably paid for your schooling with my candy habit."

She blushes and laughs, amused by the hulking lawman, calmed at once by his easy smile and air of authority. Fred looks him over, too, trying to place him, to pull his face from a mental index of thousands of customers, old and young, black and white, who'd patronized his pharmacy over the years. Grayson's close-cropped hair contains a touch of gray these days, his shoulders a bit stooped from too many nights spent poring over the bank records of drug kingpins. But Fred remembers him from a different time, when Grayson was a rail-thin, afro-sporting teenager dropping off his mother's prescriptions, buying bags of M&M's with nickels and dimes.

"Mr. M and M!" Fred says, using the nickname he'd given Grayson decades earlier. For the first time all week, the old pharmacist smiles. "You loved your candies something *fierce*."

"I'm glad you remember," Grayson says, staring out the half-shattered store windows into the street. "Seems like everything went and changed around here except this place."

"Yes, before the riots, that was true," says Fred, picking up pieces of a broken Smucker's jelly jar from the floor. "Now it's beyond changed."

To Grayson, this store's always been an integral part of what he calls "the Good Baltimore," a place where African Americans own their own businesses, generate goodwill in the community, and serve as a counterweight to murderous drug gangs. *This* is the Baltimore he's spent his career trying to cultivate; the city he believes can be a beacon of hope for the rest of black America, he says, if only its "righteous citizens" would "stand up to the killers." But, looking over the wrecked pharmacy, Grayson realizes that the bad has defeated the good yet again, that this family-owned drugstore was no match for Baltimore's criminals.

"I have every intention of finding the people who did this," Grayson tells Fred and Patti. "However long it takes."

They give him a tour of the looted store, walking him past the smashed cash register and disassembled blood pressure machine, beside which sits a large pile of human excrement.

"As if the looting wasn't enough," Patti says, "they had to insult us, too."

They show Grayson a room that once housed a safe containing hundreds of controlled substances, before looters carried that away, too.

"They really did take every drug of value," says Fred.

Patti retrieves the tape she'd pulled from the store's security camera system, sliding it into the TV/VCR her father keeps behind the pharmacy counter—a machine so old and dusty, the looters hadn't bothered with it.

"The quality isn't very good, but you can see some of the clothes, their gaits, the shapes of their bodies," Patti says. She fast-forwards a few minutes into the footage, hitting play just as a group of elementary-school-age boys smash their way through the store windows and dash inside. Three of them fill their pockets with cigarettes and candy, while a fourth squats down in the corner and relieves himself.

"Baltimore's finest," Grayson says.

Soon more rioters come into the frame, adults this time, scouring the aisles and loading up on free merchandise, everything from toilet paper and shampoo to roach traps and picture frames.

"They're trashing the place. But nobody's gone for the pills—not yet," Patti says, fast-forwarding deeper into the footage. "Then *these* guys walk in."

She presses play again as two men slink inside the store, each wearing a black ski mask, their movements unhurried. One of them is so thin, his chest appears concave. But he's tall, confident in his movements, seemingly sure of his purpose. The other intruder is shorter and heavier, the curve of his potbelly visible beneath a black, short-sleeve polo. They head straight for the pharmacy counter, riffling through shelves and drawers full of medicine, grabbing every opiate in sight. When they've picked the area clean, they lift the safe full of pricey controlled substances and haul it out the back door.

"These two, they took the bulk of the meds," Patti says. "Some other people come in later and go through what's left, but these guys, they got all the opiates."

"They knew what they were looking for," Grayson says.

"Knew exactly."

Grayson thanks Patti for cuing up the crucial moments on the tape and tells her he's impressed with her analysis.

"I hope you don't mind my asking, but do you have a law enforcement background?"

Patti laughs, a little embarrassed by the question.

"No, but my ex-husband was a PI," she says. "I got really interested in the business, started helping him out with cases. He's gone, but I still got the bug, I guess."

"Well, you did good work here," says Grayson.

"Happy to help," Patti says, smiling a smile her father hasn't seen since before her divorce.

Grayson, three years removed from his own marriage ending, hands Patti his card, promising he'll be in touch. Afterward, Fred gently ribs his daughter.

"You always go for them law-and-order types, don't you?"

"Stop it, Dad," she says, laughing.

They embrace between a pile of toppled Tide bottles, hugging each other tightly, trying to ignore the chorus of police sirens wailing outside.

Back at the Western District station, Grayson goes through hours of surveillance video, analyzing each grainy frame in search of clues—a clear face, a distinctive piece of clothing, anything that might lead him to the drugstore looters. By the next morning, he's compiled a folder thick with video still images and detailed suspect descriptions, files he emails to his colleagues in the department as well as DEA Special Agent Kirstin Marques in DC, Detective Frank Calvacca in Chicago, and Detective Jeffrey Madigan in Newark, all of whom are handling cases involving riot pills in their respective jurisdictions.

"The stills are a good start," Grayson tells his squad sergeant, Mike Malinowski, of the images. "But we're playing from behind."

In the past week, Grayson says, 13 people have overdosed on opiates in the greater Baltimore area. More than a dozen others have been seriously wounded or killed in shootings and stabbings. Grayson suspects looted drugs are behind the upticks in both and believes he must act quickly to save the lives of drug users, gang members, and civilians alike.

"If these guys are moving product at the pace they seem to be and [shooting] people at the pace we think they are, then we're going to be looking at totals this big every week . . . until they're [arrested]," he tells Malinowski.

After briefing his sergeant, Grayson meets with an array of informants across the city, looking for fresh leads. Some of Grayson's snitches are longtime junkies with 10- or 15-bag-a-day heroin habits, men and women the detective has known for years, and on whom he depends for a steady supply of under-world gossip. Other informants are new to the game, young addicts living on the streets, hoping to trade a bit of info to Grayson for 5 or 10 bucks, enough to procure a bag of heroin and maybe a spike.

Old or young, seasoned or green, all tell Grayson the same story: Mysterious, tech-savvy hustlers aligned with BGF are moving looted opiates at cut-rate prices, lower than Baltimore has ever seen. And they've got a name to match their ambition: Pill City.

"Man, I was *positive* these niggas were scamming me on that Zohydro, until I melted one down and [injected] it," says Derek Curry, the one-eyed addict who, for the last six years, has been one of Grayson's best informants. "Once it hit me, I knew they was legit."

Grayson hates seeing Curry this way: disheveled, un-healthy, perpetually high. He recalls hearing the guitarist perform at some of the top clubs in Baltimore back in the day; recalls being awed by the complexity of his riffs, the nimble-ness of his hands. Today, those same hands are covered in sores and scabs, ravaged by years of drug cooking and injec-tions, both of which intensified after his wife's overdose. As much as Grayson wishes he could cut Curry off as an informant—maybe even encourage him to enter rehab—the information he provides is just too valuable, especially now.

"How much they charging, these Pill City guys?" Grayson says. "You said low, but how low?"

"Next to nothing," says Curry, who sees his informing to Grayson not as snitching but as a kind of penance for Cassie's death, a way of saving other addicts like her, even if he refuses to stop using drugs himself. "I got me 20 Vikes the other day for 50 [dollars]. And no, you ain't hearing me wrong, Detective."

The price is laughably cheap, Grayson thinks: two dollars and change for each Vicodin pill, compared to the $30 price Jimmy Masters's dealers were charging for those same drugs before the riots.

Grayson asks where Pill City is doing most of its business, "West side or east?"

"Man, these boys are *everywhere*," Curry says, explaining that looted pills are being distributed by BGF corner crews as well as delivery men, slingers who bring opiates to customers' doors in some of the roughest parts of the city. "You just text a number and they come to you."

"Can you put in an order," Grayson says, "so I can see how they work it?"

Curry nods, whips out his phone, and asks the detective for $30 in buy money, plus a $10 "finder's fee" for himself. Cash in hand, Curry pulls a crumpled envelope from his pocket and texts the number scrawled on the back, placing an order for five Vicodin—pills that were worth $30 each before the riots. The Pill City price, Curry says, is $30 *total*.

"Every head out here's singing their praises," Curry says of the syndicate. "You got people flopping down in the street, overdosing right where they stand. And that's making folks want them pills even more."

Ten minutes later, a navy blue Caprice pulls up across the street, a known BGF member, Anthony "Deuce" Fenton, sitting behind the wheel. Grayson, hiding behind a nearby building, watches as Curry climbs in on the Caprice's passenger side and pays Deuce for the pills. Less than a minute later, he's back at Grayson's side.

"Voilá," Curry says, handing Grayson a baggie containing five Vikes. "Just like I said, ain't it?"

Grayson looks closely at the pills, touches his tongue to one of them, and knows right away they're the real thing. He asks Curry why other dealers are allowing an upstart drug crew to operate in this area. After all, doesn't the block they're standing on still fall within the far-reaching territories of Jimmy Masters?

"This *was* Jimmy's block, before these BGF niggas started dropping bodies," Curry says. "Jimmy's people hurting out here, for real. They fading."

The efficiency, the ruthlessness, the soaring body count; all of it's enough to make Grayson wonder what he's up against. He thanks Curry and returns to the Western District station, certain now that he's dealing with a new kind of drug operation, unlike any Baltimore's seen.

"Forget about 'Good Baltimore' and 'Bad Baltimore,'" he tells Malinowski that afternoon. "This one's a different breed."

"Boulevards of Pain"

Am I willing to die for my addiction? Absolutely.

—TAMARA SWINTON

They call it Oxy Alley.

On first glance, it looks like any other blighted street in West Baltimore, filled with vacant rowhomes, discarded liquor bottles, and addicts stumbling out of the corner carry-outs, looking like the zombies from Michael Jackson's *Thriller* video. But a closer look at this run-down stretch of Pennsylvania Avenue reveals something more troubling, for in nearly every vacant, opiate addicts are getting high on looted Pill City product.

Two such users, Keisha Jones, 23, and Terry Augman, 21, are holed up in one of those roach-infested rowhomes, boiling down a batch of looted pills into liquid form. Keisha's six-year-old son, Moises, sits in the corner playing with his Hess truck while the women, friends since high school, speculate about the quality of the drugs they're about to inject.

"Going to be real nice," Keisha says, melting the oxycodone with a lighter and spoon while Terry readies a syringe. "These them Black Ivorys, 40s [milligrams]."

"I just hope they're as good as them Hollywoods," says Terry, who's recently learned she's six weeks pregnant with her first child. She hasn't seen the baby's father, her ex-boyfriend, Tyrone Moxley, in five.

"I got to make the most of this today, because I can't be fooling around with [pills] no more," Terry says. "The BIs [Black Ivorys] got to be my send-off."

Pill City gives memorable names to all its opiates, "brands" that change every few weeks and vary based on the type of drug and dosage. F-16s, Hollywoods, Bodymores, Yellowcakes, Mike Tysons, Black Dominoes, and Red Tails were all the rage in late April. In early May, it was Pinkies, Blue Angels, and Dark Knights every addict wanted. Now it's Beyoncés and Black Ivorys they're clamoring for.

"Them BGF niggas ain't let us down yet, have they?" says Keisha, who, like Terry, first began abusing pain pills earlier this month, procuring them from BGF member Train Lockwood. "I'm sure they done right by us with these, too."

In other vacants along Oxy Alley, there are addicts just like them, people snorting and shooting opiates from dusk till dawn, many of whom got their product from Jimmy Masters's dealers before Pill City came along. The concentration of drug abusers on this street is among the highest in the country— casualties of the ongoing wave of urban opiate addiction, overdose, and associated violence ravaging America's inner cities with little notice from wealthier enclaves. Few outside the game ever venture to Oxy Alley or streets like it, viewing them as places "beyond redemption," says Chris Sheehan, a Baltimore homicide detective who's investigating a number of killings in the area.

"You come here for one of three reasons: to buy drugs, to sell drugs, or because you just don't care anymore and . . . don't mind dying," Sheehan says. "The only other excuse is that you're a [homicide or narcotics] detective."

Addicts along the alley tend to agree.

"I fuck for pills, I steal for pills, I break into houses for pills, whatever I need to do get my pills, I do it, just like everybody else around here," says Vanessa Jackson, 37, who's snorting a pair of Vikes three houses down from Keisha and Terry, just as a series of gunshots ring out in the distance. "That's our soundtrack," Jackson jokes.

The former beautician says she'd never touched anything harder than marijuana before the riots, taking heed of the lessons she'd learned watching heroin ruin the lives of siblings, cousins, neighbors, and customers at the beauty shop where she once worked.

"After everything got so crazy around here, with Freddie Gray and all that, I was feeling real bad," Jackson explains. "I heard those BGF boys touting cheap pills . . . saying they as good as heroin, but a lot safer. So I did the stupid thing, went and texted them. From then on they brought me [pills] every day, long as I got cash or I'm down [to have sex]."

Since then, Jackson's lost her job, seen her longtime boyfriend end their relationship, and been arrested multiple times for drug possession.

"But the thing is, I still can't stop [using]," she says.

Five houses down from where Jackson's getting high, Roderick Hess, 44, has just finished injecting two melted-down OxyContins—his drug of choice now that Pill City is supplying him with discounted painkillers by the pocketful.

"I used to use H [heroin], but H is a street drug, you know? Like an ugly, broke-down car," says Hess, who spends about $50 a day on pills. "But Oxy? Oxy's a drug like a Mercedes-Benz, something classy. If you can afford the classy one, why keep buying the one that's broke down?"

A similar analogy is drawn by Derek Curry, who's currently spending about $60 a day on pills and heroin sold by Pill City. He says he'd always thought painkillers were "mainly for white people, people with a little money and good insurance. Because folks like me can't usually afford them." Indeed, studies have shown prescribers are far less likely to give opiate painkillers to African Americans, due largely to racial bias.

"It was always hard to get my hands on them," Curry says. "They were scarce."

But that changed after the riots.

"Pills ain't never been big as heroin around here, until Pill City *made* them big," says Curry. "Lot of people done switched [from heroin to pills] after them looted pills went on sale. This always been a heroin town, though."

Baltimore has been American's heroin capital since the 1960s, registering the highest per capita addiction rate of any large municipality in the country as recently as 2014. That year, the local department of health counted at least 60,000 drug addicts in the city, as many as 48,000 of them addicted to heroin. By some estimates, 1 of every 10 residents living in the city is a heroin addict, "and even that sounds low to me," says Curry.

Given its long history with heroin addiction, Baltimore in 2015 is, in many ways, the "natural epicenter" of America's inner-city opiate scourge, says Kirstin Marques, the DEA agent.

"If the white kid dying in his bedroom in the suburbs is a

symbol of the first wave," Marques says, "Oxy Alley on Penn [Pennsylvania Avenue] is a symbol for the second."

But opiates are only one part of the problem, she says.

The April riots laid bare obstacles faced by Baltimore's most vulnerable black residents: poverty, gun violence, social isolation, substandard housing, vacant properties, failing schools, unconstitutional policing, and overincarceration. But they also made many of these problems worse, leading to diminished economic activity, surging crime, an influx of looted opiates, and a corresponding surge in addiction.

It's not just happening in Baltimore, either. Across the country, new Oxy Alleys are cropping up with numbing frequency, turning blighted streets into what Marques calls "boulevards of pain." The people overdosing in these areas are mostly impoverished and mostly black, records show. Among them: a 24-year-old hairdresser in St. Louis raising two kids on her own; a 20-year-old short order cook in Chicago with dreams of attending a major university; a 46-year-old janitor in Milwaukee with five children to support; and an adult education teacher in Philadelphia with dreams of moving to the suburbs. In Camden, Chicago, New Orleans, Cincinnati, Detroit, Atlanta, and other cities, dozens more are entering hospitals, rehab clinics, and morgue freezers every day.

"Do I know I'm probably going to die for my addiction? Absolutely," says Tamara Swinton, a Pill City customer living in New Orleans' Lower Ninth Ward, the same neighborhood ravaged by Hurricane Katrina in 2005. "But right now, the pills are what I need. So I keep using."

Keisha Jones and Terry Augman, who have never traveled outside Baltimore City, were unlucky enough to be among Pill City's first customers. Like other new users, they'd heard about looted opiates selling at discount prices and thought, "Why not see what they're about?" Keisha recalls.

The drugs had to be safer than heroin, the women assumed, since "that junk is strictly for lowlifes and fiends," Keisha remembers thinking. But pills? If the price was right and they took the edge off, the women saw no reason to abstain.

"I thought they would make me feel better," says Terry, scanning her scar-covered arms in search of an untapped vein. "And lord knows, they have. It's the best feeling, you know, because it makes you feel so confident, so at ease. It makes you feel like everything's right."

As Terry elaborates on her love for opiates, Moises, still seated in corner, calls out to Keisha.

"Can we please go, Mommy?' he says, growing tired of sitting in the damp, dark vacant.

The women are so caught up in preparing their oxy for injection, they'd forgotten all about the boy. Not that they mind using in front of him.

By now, Keisha says, he's used to it.

"Not yet, love," she says. "Mommy's busy."

As poor, black residents of a violence-plagued, inner-city neighborhood, both Keisha and Terry fall squarely within Pill City's target demographic. Keisha is a single mother living well beneath the poverty line, while Terry typically resides in a women's shelter. They work part-time at a discount clothing store in Baltimore, snorting or injecting 10 to 12 pills a day in the employee bathroom.

"I think maybe I'd have gotten some help by now," Terry says, "if I knew where to start."

If the friends were living in a more prosperous neighborhood, statistics suggest, they'd have a significantly better chance of getting treatment. Data shows most government-funded outreach and rehab programs in U.S. inner cities are severely underfunded, meaning a poor black opiate addict is less likely than a better-off white one to get the help he or she needs, experts say.

Baltimore's health commissioner, Dr. Leana Wen, highlighted the problem in testimony to the U.S. House of Representatives Oversight and Government Reform Committee, describing the difficulties faced by inner-city residents looking to kick opiates.

"I remember well my patient, a 24-year-old mother of two who came to the ER nearly every week requesting addiction treatment," Wen, a former practicing physician, recalled. "She would be told there was nowhere for her to go that day or the next, and would be offered an appointment in three weeks' time. Because she lacked housing and other supportive services, she would relapse. One day, her family found her unresponsive and not breathing. By the time she arrived in the ER, it was too late for us to save her, and she died."

Dr. Marcus Elgion, a Baltimore-based physician specializing in addiction treatment, says the dearth of quality rehab options in inner cities is "just one of the many ways black opiate abusers are treated differently from whites suffering from the same disease. In white suburbs and rural spaces, there are shortages, too, but there is also outrage at those shortages. Not so in poor communities of color."

Elgion's seen the impact of riot pills and heroin firsthand—not only on addicts at a well-known Baltimore hospital, where he's a doctor in residency, but also in his own family. Elgion's estranged father, Morris Elgion, 63, died of an opiate overdose in late April 2015 in his Pigtown apartment. Two weeks later,

Morris's wife, Shanise, 56, committed suicide with a mix of vodka and opiate painkillers. Later, a teenager Elgion mentored would be wounded by a BGF gunman in Penn-North.

"Why is there disparate treatment for blacks suffering during this epidemic and for the people suffering from related violence in our communities?" Elgion asks. "For whatever reason, the white addict is more often seen as an unwilling, innocent victim of doctors and drug companies, and that's colored the way society views them: as victims, people suffering from disease, people who need a second chance." But black, inner-city opiate abusers, especially heroin addicts, "are still seen by politicians, the media, and the public as being somehow complicit in their addictions and therefore not deserving of the same sympathy [as whites]," Elgion says. "It's a staggering double standard, when you think about it."

Elgion, who is African American, says racism is just one factor contributing to that disparate treatment. Also at play is "the lack of political influence among poor blacks living in drug-plagued neighborhoods, and the limited number of treatment options in those places when compared to white communities," the doctor says. "Both of those factors mean there's less visibility for black addicts, and, therefore, less awareness and corresponding empathy in society."

Rita Wexler, a New Orleans physician specializing in addiction treatment, sees another culprit: black market pain pills. These days, she says, opiate dealing organizations like Pill City aren't just distributors of stolen drugs; they're purchasers, too. The BGF franchise in New Orleans, for example, serves as a kind of clearinghouse for pharmacy robbers looking to unload their illicit hauls, says Wexler. After ripping off a drug store, a perpetrator can sell pain pills to BGF at their street value; an arrangement that's turned Pill City into one of the largest known sellers *and* buyers of stolen opiates in America.

"When the first wave of opiate addicts found their pill supply choked off by [law enforcement] crackdowns and government regulations, they switched to heroin, since it offers the same high as pain pills but, at 5 or 10 bucks a bag, is a lot cheaper," says Wexler. "Pill City essentially turned that dynamic on its head. They made pills affordable to poor minorities, even as whites were increasingly being priced out of that market and switching to heroin. And now, [BGF] are the guys you come to when you have product you want to unload."

While data compiled by the Centers for Disease Control and Prevention suggests whites who get their pills from doctors are dying at a higher rate than blacks, CDC records, federal autopsy statistics, law enforcement filings, and public health data from America's 10 largest cities indicate that opiates sold on the black market—including stolen drugs peddled by Pill City—are killing African Americans in higher numbers than whites.

"With regard to overdose deaths caused by illicit opiates, black users are suffering disproportionally, based on what we're seeing in African American communities right now," says Elgion. "That we don't hear more about them speaks volumes about the dialogue surrounding addiction in this country. When the data only reflects one side of the story, only one group gets the media attention and financial resources."

Journalists in the United States have focused on white opiate users "to the detriment of blacks, who are seeing more resources funneled to whiter areas," says Christina Keller, an addiction counselor in Cleveland, Ohio, where BGF has flooded impoverished pockets of the city with pills and heroin.

"It's not being done maliciously, but rather because wealthier rural and suburban white communities know how to make their voices heard when it comes to opiate abuse," Keller says. "The squeaky wheel gets the grease. In this case, the grease is news coverage and the government funding that follows it."

As an example of one-sided coverage, Keller cites a January 2016 *New York Times* article on mortality rates, which stated that "researchers repeatedly speculate that the nation is seeing a cohort of whites who are isolated and left out of the economy and society and who have gotten ready access to cheap heroin and to prescription narcotic drugs."

"Talk about isolated and left out of the economy . . . that's how black communities have felt since this country's inception!" exclaims Keller, who is white. "There's no question white opiate addicts are suffering in an unprecedented way due to some of these same conditions, but we cannot ignore the fact that there are African Americans living this way, too. My question is: Where are the stories about them?"

As for Pill City, many of its associates say they're grateful for the lack of press scrutiny.

"If our customers were white, that shit would be on the front page," Damage says. "That would make doing what we do . . . a lot harder."

For all the success Pill City's had, it's hardly the first business to make a fortune off of opiates.

"It's been happening for over 100 years, with everyone from Bayer to Purdue Pharma to Pill City cashing in," says Wexler. "Making money off of opiate addiction is American as apple pie."

Bayer, the drug company Wexler calls "the inventor of the addiction-industrial complex," began selling heroin in the

1890s, marketing the drug as a nonaddictive cough medicine. Bayer's tactics would later be imitated by a group Elgion calls "our country's legal pushers"; the modern pharmaceutical companies that fueled America's first wave of opiate pill addiction between roughly 2000 and 2014. Leading the charge was Purdue Pharma, which earned billions marketing its oxycodone-based pain pill, OxyContin, as safe and largely nonaddictive.

As Purdue's profits soared, competing drug makers ramped up production of their own opiates. Predictably, the fallout was catastrophic: Between 2000 and 2010, the number of opiate prescriptions written in America quadrupled, as did overdose deaths over the same period. The federal government recorded 4,030 fatal opiate overdoses in 2000. Ten years later, that number reached 16,651.

And it kept getting worse.

In 2012, 259 million opiate pain medication prescriptions were written by health care professionals, the most of any nation in the world. In 2014, 18,893 Americans died of prescription opiate overdoses—the highest annual total on record.

Today, approximately 1.9 million Americans abuse prescription opiates while roughly 1.5 million suffer from heroin addiction, government research shows.

"These drug companies who started all this, they were essentially dealers who didn't need guns," says Keller. "They had marketing instead, and pharmaceutical reps, and lawyers, and hundreds of doctors in their pocket, backing them up. They put us in a terrible place as a country.

"But," she adds, "it wasn't always like this."

Before the late 1990s, prescription opiates in America were reserved almost exclusively for cancer patients and end-of-life care. Since synthetic opiates like oxycodone are chemically similar to heroin, most doctors considered them too powerful—

and addictive—to prescribe. Then, in the mid-1990s, things started to change. A small but vocal group of pain specialists and patient advocacy groups began arguing for wider use of opiate painkillers, penning editorials, lobbying politicians, and propagating research they said proved these pills were safe. The crux of their argument: Chronic pain patients were needlessly suffering, when the treatment they needed, prescription opiates, ought to be just a doctor's visit away.

The campaign worked. Government rules regulating opiate prescribing were soon eased, allowing doctors to give these powerful pills not just to cancer patients but to anyone complaining of pain, be it a sore back or migraine headache.

"That," Elgion says, "was the beginning of the end."

When Purdue Pharma introduced OxyContin in 1996, it marketed the drug as safe replacement for existing painkillers, insisting that the drug's time-release formula—which doled out an opiate payload over the course of several hours rather than all at once—made it difficult to abuse. The chances of a patient becoming addicted to OxyContin was minuscule, "less than 1 percent," Purdue claimed. Yet users quickly found ways to scuttle the drug's delayed-release formulation. By breaking up a pill and snorting it—or melting it down and taking it intravenously—a user got the daily opiate payload all at once, rendering the safety feature useless.

Many users learned too late how dangerous the drug could be when injected. Among them was Derek Curry, whose wife died of an OxyContin overdose inside their Gwynn Oak home in Baltimore. Curry howled for someone to save her, but paramedics arrived too late, and the painkiller in her bloodstream was simply too potent.

"I've lived through every phase of this [epidemic], going

from heroin to pills, then back to heroin, and now to heroin *and* pills," Curry says. "But for my wife, man, pills was where it was at. She loved them. And that OC [OxyContin] was the killer."

In 2007, Purdue pleaded guilty to federal charges of misleading physicians and the public about the risk of abuse and addiction posed by OxyContin, admitting that "some employees made, or told other employees to make, certain statements about OxyContin to some health care professionals that were inconsistent with the FDA-approved prescribing information."

Still, sales of OxyContin continued to boom, reaching $3.1 billion in 2010. Meanwhile, rival companies kept churning out their own oxycodone-based painkillers in record-breaking numbers. The DEA approved the manufacturing of 149,375 kilograms of oxycodone in 2014—42 times the amount made in 1993, according to journalist John Temple's book *American Pain*. In 2015, the DEA authorized production of 137,500 kilograms of oxycodone—a 39-fold increase over the span of 22 years, Temple reports.

Over the past six years, the DEA has pursued fewer cases against drug makers, pharmacies, distributors, and doctors—a trend many experts attribute to increased lobbying by the pharmaceutical industry.

"It's like we're going backwards, putting more drugs out there when we should be scaling back," says Wexler. "How many of those pills are going to end up in poor black areas, without anyone noticing but the people in those neighborhoods? So many, it's a crime."

Amid the boom in American opiate production, Mexican drug cartels have had to scramble to keep up. Sinaloa, the largest and richest of these organizations, is smuggling more illegal product into America than any cartel in history—heroin that's purer, cheaper, and more powerful than any the DEA has seen. The cartel and its competitors "have had to up their game" to compete with American pharmaceutical companies whose opiates offer "a cleaner, purer opiate high" that can "give even the best heroin a run for its money," says Marques. As a result, the number of deadly heroin overdoses nationwide is soaring, as are deaths caused by fentanyl, with which Mexican heroin is frequently cut.

Transnational drug cartels and pharmaceutical companies alike are thriving these days, with high-tech, inner-city operations like Pill City not far behind. The encrypted syndicate, Marques says, "is just the latest step in that evolution . . . that process of profiting off of people's pain and addiction with increasingly creative methods."

"Sinners"

> *To Five-O, y'all ain't no different from any man hustling dope.*
>
> —Damage

Pill City's franchises are getting so many drug orders, they can't keep up.

In Kansas City and St. Louis, BGF leaders are texting Lyric and Damage every few hours, begging for a re-up. In Camden, Newark, and Staten Island, they're texting Train to say they've never sold so much dope or pills so quickly, begging him to send more. The approximately $100 million worth of opiates stolen in Baltimore are spreading through impoverished inner-city neighborhoods "like a virus," says Marques, "going places we really didn't expect them to go."

Tonight, she's seeing that damage firsthand in the form of opiate addicts all over the nation's capital, some nodding off on sidewalks, others in run-down project stairwells. Marques shakes a few of them awake and asks them where they're getting their drugs.

"Texted for 'em," one man slurs.

"Got them from a delivery boy, sold them to me for cheap," says another man, calling it the "Baltimore discount."

Later, Marques calls Grayson with an update on her findings. The DEA and Baltimore police are working closely together these days to try to nab drug looters. And both agencies are alarmed by what their investigators are seeing.

"I can't walk two blocks without finding people high on BGF product," she says.

"Tell me about it," says Grayson. "I'm getting calls from half the PDs on the Eastern Seaboard and [Midwest], saying their ODs are up. And guess who they're blaming? B'More."

They discuss the various leads they're working: tips about Pill City's founders being little more than children; rumors about a power struggle within the upper ranks of BGF; and talk that Jimmy Masters's syndicate is on the verge of collapse, under increasing pressure from BGF. By the time they're done commiserating, it's after 10 p.m., too late for Grayson to call Patti Sinclair and ask her out to dinner, something he's been planning to do for weeks now.

"Keep me posted," Marques tells Grayson before hanging up. "And don't stress too much. We're going to catch these guys. Just a matter of when."

The next morning, June 1, Damage stops by Brick and Wax's office space, the BGF field marshal one of the few people who knows where to find the teens these days. The programmers have vowed to spend as little time in public as possible, hoping to decrease their chances of getting arrested.

"Damn, looks like the mothafucking Bates Motel up in here," Damage says, taking in the dreary décor. Other than the high-priced electronics, makeshift desks, and hacker dictums posted on the walls, the space is bare, unless you count the rat droppings, dead cockroaches, and bevy of spiderwebs.

"With all the bugs we got crawling around, we never get lonely," jokes Wax.

The gangsters are listening to Kendrick Lamar's *Good Kid, M.A.A.D. City*, the album blasting from Brick's computer speakers while he and Wax pound away on their respective keyboards, writing the code that's helping to keep dozens of impoverished African American neighborhoods awash in opiates. Hunched over their monitors, wearing untucked dress shirts and jeans, they look more like Silicon Valley cubicle jockeys than drug traffickers. Only instead of coding manuals, they've got high-caliber pistols resting on their desks.

"I don't really give a fuck if people think we're criminals, because what we're doing, it's never been done," Brick tells his cousin after Damage hands him a *Baltimore Sun* article about the government's probe of the pharmacy lootings. "The truth is, we're programmers. And we're doing work that most [programmers] only wish they could do."

"Y'all may *think* that," says Damage. "But to Five-O, y'all ain't no different from any man hustling dope."

Brick and Wax tell Damage they're still processing all that's happened to them, "especially the fact that, basically, we're rich," Wax says. Indeed, after a long afternoon of programming and troubleshooting issues involving their Dark Web drug marketplace, the duo learns exactly how wealthy they are when they tally the latest wave of illicit profits delivered by Damage. Piling foot-high stacks of cash upon their desks, their mouths slightly agape, the teens look at each other in disbelief. It's more money than they'd anticipated, the boys say. A *lot* more.

"I didn't expect to see numbers like this so soon, for real," says Wax, punching profit totals into a spreadsheet on his computer, one of several databases he's created to track the operation's earnings, supply levels, and expenditures.* "They're huge."

"And they only going to get bigger," says Damage. "If we made this in a month, imagine what we can pull down in a year."

In its first five weeks of operation, the syndicate has netted over half a million dollars in cash, $170,000 of which is sitting on Brick and Wax's desks, the rest of which is being divvied up among BGF franchises. It's a fantastic sum for two project-reared kids, neither of whom ever laid eyes on anything bigger than a $20 bill before the riots.

"Now all we need is a nicer place to work," Wax says.

"For real, maybe we can get y'all some office space downtown," says Damage.

"Nah, yo, this right here is all we need," Brick says, pointing to the room full of computers. "Don't matter if it's in Cali or Baltimore. The gear's what matters."

The syndicate, Brick explains, is using some of the same algorithmic and analytic technologies popularized by Google, Amazon, and Facebook, its computers analyzing thousands of data points every hour—information drawn from federal census records, online court documents, news stories, public health statistics, and government databases. Among their many uses, these algorithms track policing patterns in hundreds of U.S. neighborhoods, then steer BGF dealers clear of streets where cops are concentrated. They also identify what Brick calls "hot markets"—places where young, low-income

---

* Several databases were shown to this reporter, in order to help corroborate the syndicate leaders' claims.

African Americans are clustered—as destructive a tool that's ever existed in the urban drug game, authorities say. The technology even helps BGF franchises find new territories, which means the syndicate can do more damage in more communities. Or, as Wax says with a straight face: "It allows us to quickly serve customers where they live and work."

"I like the way that sounds, yo," says Brick. "You talking more like one of them Cali boys all the time."

Later, when Damage and Wax make a run to the carry-out for lunch, this reporter calls Brick to ask how he got his nickname.

"You really want to know?" he asks. "'Cause that shit ain't easy on the stomach."

The story, he says, begins on a sunny afternoon in mid-2008, a few months after he'd first met Wax. Walking home from school that day, he says he spotted a brownish red brick laying in the street, one of its corners chipped, by happenstance, to an iceberg-shape point. It gave James, then 11, an idea, he says, one he'd contemplated many times before but always lacked the courage to execute.

This is it, he says he told himself that afternoon, picking up the brick and placing it in his backpack. *I can do this*.

In his room that night, he practiced swinging the jagged brick again and again, repeating the motion until his shoulder grew sore. Then he slid under the covers, trying to keep his courage up, counting the minutes till sunrise. To kill time, he reminisced about going to church with his mom, about all the "pointless" praying he'd done to keep Arthur away.

The door creaked just after 9 a.m.

James pretended to be asleep, nuzzling his head into a pillow, his back turned to the door. He heard Arthur's heavy breathing, smelled his rank aftershave. And as his mother's boyfriend climbed beneath the covers, James reached for his crude weapon.

The first blow knocked Arthur out cold.

"How that feel?" James said, striking his abuser again and again, stopping only when he'd exhausted himself.

Afterward, he tried to locate Arthur's pulse but felt nothing. *It's over,* he thought.

But in truth, James's trials were just beginning.

"What did you do?" his mother howled when she saw Arthur's body.

Renata had slept through her boyfriend's murder but not the sound of her son trying to drag him out the front door, toward the dumpster out back.

"I had to do it," James said, Arthur's corpse still wedged in the doorway. "He wasn't never going to stop."

Around that time, a passing neighbor glimpsed the macabre scene and, returning to his apartment, called 911. Renata, hearing police sirens in the distance, injected a large dose of heroin, then nodded off on the couch.

The first officer to arrive roused her, asking what happened.

"I killed him," Renata said, groggy but coherent.

"*You* killed him?" the officer said, looking skeptically at her bony frame, emaciated from years of drug abuse and malnourishment. Behind him, several cops were securing the crime scene, careful not to touch Arthur's body.

"Yes, sir," Renata said, pointing to the blood-soaked brick lying in the corner. "He wouldn't give me the drugs he owed me, so I killed him with that."

The homicide detectives who worked the case didn't believe Renata's story—they saw the blood splashed on her son's clothes, the indentations from the brick etched into his palm. But James insisted he was innocent, and Renata's confession made the case a slam dunk. They booked her on a charge of second-degree murder. The next night, she was sitting in the Baltimore City Detention Center, dope sick and depressed.

Without her head pills—the drugs Renata took to keep her bipolar disorder under control—she soon lapsed into a major depressive downswing. It's not clear whether she told corrections officers she needed psychiatric treatment, but friends say her mental health worsened by the day, until she "couldn't really function."

After six weeks in the jail, she got hold of a hot shot of heroin—a lethal dose laced with poison—and committed suicide. Guards found her cold to the touch in her cell, a palm-size photo of her son stashed under her pillow.

"So that's why they call me Brick," the programmer turned kingpin says. "Nothing more to it."

"What about the funeral?" this reporter asks.

"Shit, you taking me waaaaaay back."

Renata's memorial, he explains, was held at a storefront church in Cherry Hill a week after her death, presided over by a drug dealer turned street preacher named Marvin Grier. A fiery orator, Grier—who'd never been officially ordained—ministered to the poor, addicted, and otherwise downtrodden, using his pulpit to criticize those still involved in the drug game, especially the Black Guerrilla Family. He made a habit of eulogizing locals whose lives were lost to heroin, too, his powerful voice and piercing green eyes allowing him to "hold people in the palm of his hand when he spoke, because they truly believed God had sent him," a fellow preacher recalled.

"Even the worst sinners among us can find redemption in

Christ, *if* we repent," Grier told the handful of mourners gathered to remember Renata that morning in 2008, including James and Willie. "Even killers can save their souls, if they seek forgiveness. And I truly believe Renata did before she passed."

Like most others in attendance, Grier believed Renata, not her son, killed Arthur Kane. But her sin seemed to make not a bit of difference to Grier, for he believed in the concept of "redemption without question," he said, "so long as one's heart is not evil."

What God *wouldn't* forgive, Grier told the mourners, was the "kind of evil-hearted hustlers" who'd "ruined Renata's life," and those of so many other Baltimoreans. It was a subject the preacher knew plenty about, given his background. He'd been convicted of heroin trafficking in the late 1960s, caught while unloading a drug shipment in Southern California. During his incarceration at San Quentin State Prison, he became friendly with George Jackson, an ex–Black Panther who'd founded BGF as a black revolutionary group. Grier joined the organization, found religion, renounced drug dealing, and became a Black Power activist. He broke with BGF only after one of its members, a drug dealer named Tyrone Robinson, assassinated the Black Panther cofounder Huey Newton in 1989.

"We are all terribly flawed and in need of mercy," Grier said toward the end of Renata's service, staring hard at James in the front row, as if anticipating the horrors to come. "And today, even the most wicked among us must humbly repent."

Walking back to Willie's after the burial, James felt like Grier had "seen right through me." He wondered if he could be forgiven—not just for taking a life, but for letting his mother take the fall for Arthur's murder. He no longer cared what God thought, he said, not after what he'd let Arthur do to him. But he also didn't want to spend eternity in hell, especially if Arthur was going to be there.

"Hey, Willie, I got to tell you something," James said, a few blocks south of the shooting gallery where they'd first met. "I did that to Arthur, not my moms."

"For real?"

"Yeah, for real," James said, tears in his eyes. "I had to make him stop, didn't I?"

"Definitely, yo," Willie said, hugging his best friend. "You did what you had to do."

The boys had grown closer since Renata's arrest, James moving in with Willie and his mom in order "to keep my head down and hide" from the child welfare workers he knew were searching for him. James loved it there in the dingy two-bedroom in Gilmor, spending his evenings playing *Grand Theft Auto* on Willie's secondhand PlayStation or devouring books from the public library. Brenda Harris was rarely home in those days, working the streets to feed, clothe, and keep a roof over all three of their heads.

Living at Willie's, James was "finally feeling good about things," he says, the boys forging a bond that seemed unbreakable. They started their first business venture that year, doing their classmates' homework assignments for $5 a pop. Both were spending more time online, too, posting on various blogs and tech discussion groups, learning how to code.

In Willie, James believed he'd finally found someone who "got me," he says—a fellow reader, tech lover, and junior entrepreneur. He planned to live with his best friend as long as he could and eventually start a "serious company" with him.

But first, Willie said, James needed a nickname.

"Sorry, yo, but James? That sound kind of nerdy on the Internet."

"Aight, so give me one, then."

Willie weighed the possibilities for a few minutes.

"I'mma call you Brick," he said at last. "'Cause that's how you changed shit up."

The name matched nicely, James thought, with the nickname Willie himself had recently been given. A fellow programmer saw some code the 11-year-old had posted on a message board and declared that he'd "waxed it," another way of saying he'd mastered the task. Hence, the programmer said, he would call him Wax.

"Brick and Wax, I like the sound of that," James said as they surfed the Web that night. "Those names going to ring out someday."

PART II

JIMMY'S WORLD

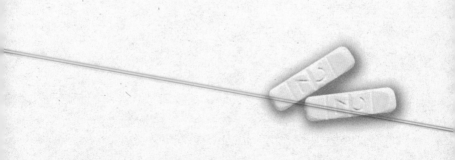

"Supercartel"

It ain't over till they close the coffin.

—Jimmy Masters

The bodies keep piling up.

From the poorest stretches of Atlanta and South Florida, to the most neglected sections of Chicago and Los Angeles, BGF franchises are decimating local gangs while flooding many of America's worst slums with high-dose opiates. In the last week of May, BGF ups the stakes yet again, going after none other than Jimmy Masters's son, Stephan "Stacks" Masters. The 41-year-old dealer is heir to an underworld empire that's spanned three generations and includes dozens of well-known gang leaders, enforcers, and drug traffickers, not just in Baltimore but throughout the American Midwest and South.

Tonight, though, he's just another gangster in Pill City's way.

"Don't stop hitting him until I say so," Slim Robinson says.

Stacks is drifting in an out of consciousness, trying in vain to protect his head as Slim and four other BGF members pummel him with boot heels, brass knuckles, and a Louisville Slugger baseball bat. He's just the latest member of his father's syndicate to be robbed of drugs since the riots, targets of an unprecedented wave of stickups, beatings, and murders perpetrated by BGF.

Yet the targeting of Stacks, Jimmy's elder son, is far from routine; it signals an escalation of BGF's gangland offensive, a wave of attacks that left at least 13 dead and 34 wounded across Baltimore in May alone, helping to make it the deadliest month the city's seen in over 40 years. By year's end, the conflict between Pill City and competing dealers will account for at least 32* of Baltimore's record-setting 344 homicides, making it one of the bloodiest underworld battles ever documented in the city.

"We told your ass to stop slinging out here," Slim tells Stacks, standing over the underworld scion as he gasps for air. The gangster's eyes are nearly swollen shut, but he still manages to spot the pistol in Slim's waistband.

"Y'all don't need to do this, for real," Stacks mumbles, spitting a cracked, blood-soaked tooth onto the pavement, the result of a well-aimed Timberland heel to his jaw.

"Afraid we do," says Slim. "Whatever peace you got to make, best make it now."

Stacks mumbles a short prayer, "Jesus Christ" the only words that are audible. Then, without another word, Slim pulls the Kel-Tec P-11 9-millimeter pistol from his waistband and fires four shots—two into Stacks's chest, two others into his head. Trails of smoke rise from each of the dime-size bullet holes, the stench of singed flesh and gunpowder filling the air.

---

* This total is based on the author's analysis of police reports and court records as well as interviews with law enforcement officials, gang members, and families of homicide victims.

Afterward, Slim reaches into Stacks's jeans pocket and removes a zip-lock bag packed with more than 200 prescription opiates—the latest bounty collected on Pill City's behalf.

"Nobody in Jimmy's world get no passes from now on, not even his sons," Slim says as he and his men lift the corpse into the back of Slim's Mercedes G Class SUV, then drive off to ditch the body outside city limits. "We going all out on them niggas, to the last man."

Two weeks after Stacks's death, his grieving father, Jimmy Masters, is standing on his syndicate's original drug corner, running a hand through his thinning gray hair.

"How," the aging kingpin says, "could we let this happen?"

Jimmy and his nephew, Kenny "Mondo" Mack, are surveying a desolate stretch of sidewalk along North Paca Street, an area that Jimmy's father, Emmanuel, first turned into a hub for heroin dealing back in 1978. It's one of at least 31 pieces of turf Masters's men have lost to BGF since the riots, a territorial yield with no known precedent in the urban underworld.

"We weren't ready for them boys, plain and simple," says Mondo, who also serves as Jimmy's bodyguard and security chief.

"To do Stacks like that, though . . . it ain't right," says Masters, who, despite the 80-plus-degree heat, is decked out in a navy blue, single-breasted bespoke suit, along with a blood-red silk tie. The syndicate boss often jokes about being past his prime, yet he still cuts an imposing figure: tall and broad-shouldered, sharply dressed, his face bearing a striking resemblance to that of the singer Ronald Isley. And while his temper isn't what it once was, the crime boss remains capable of spectacular acts of violence. Just six months ago, he'd fatally shot an employee he'd caught stealing from his organization.

A year before that, he'd nearly choked a card player to death in his illegal gambling den. The man's offense: trying to cheat Jimmy in a poker game.

But fierce as Masters is, his syndicate is no match for Pill City, which boasts more than 300 BGF members and associates across the country, outnumbering Jimmy's employees by nearly 10 to 1. In addition to killing Stacks and other Masters Organization members, Pill City has taken millions of dollars' worth of pills and heroin from their corner dealers and stash houses, decimating what was once a highly profitable opiate-dealing operation. In the face of Pill City's unceasing assault, Masters had gone into hiding, believing he could "wait out" BGF's enforcers, he says.

But in response to his son's murder, the kingpin has re-emerged and forged a plan to retaliate.

"It ain't over till they close the coffin on me, as my pops used to say," Masters explains.

He instructs Mondo to reach out to the leaders of the Gangster Disciples, Highlandtown Soldiers, Purple City, and several local Bloods sets, wanting to know whether "they'll tool up with us" against Pill City. These gangs—some of Baltimore's biggest—operate under a long-standing agreement with Masters, buying high-quality heroin and marijuana from his organization, then selling those drugs at a significant markup in their own territories. Given his existing relationship with the groups, Masters has reason to believe they'll help him take on the encrypted syndicate.

"If they won't," he says, "we'll have to make them see the light."

In late June, 20 or so gangsters gather in the back room of Jimmy's gambling hall in Ellwood Park. He makes a quick scan of their faces, noting the presence of some of Baltimore's most ruthless underworld figures. Among them are Lonnie "Eight Tray" Robertson, a high-ranking, 26-year-old member of the West Side Gangster Disciples, whose coke-dealing operations and extortion rackets have made him a millionaire several times over; Quentin "Qwiz" Cunningham, 25, member of the Highlandtown Soldiers, who started out as a corner boy before working his way to the top of his gang; and Edward "Tyson Ed" Sperry, a senior member of the Purple City gang, one of the craftiest, most violent crews in the city.

Each gangster has brought a handful of deputies along, plus some heavily armed enforcers, just in case the summit takes an unexpected turn. Based on his conciliatory words, though, Jimmy means them no harm. He says he wants to forge a coalition to fight Pill City; a "supercartel," as he calls it, that will rub the tech-savvy syndicate out of existence.

"It'll be easier for us to do this together than fight them piecemeal," he says.

Under his plan, the gangs would share "intelligence and re-sources," working together to track down and assassinate Pill City's most senior members, including its elusive cofounders, known only by their nicknames, Brick and Wax. After taking control of BGF's inventory, Masters explains, the gangs would sell the reclaimed drugs and share the profits equally.

"We can have things back to normal in two months, maybe three."

But Jimmy's prediction doesn't change what the gangsters in the room already know: that the old man is slowing down, losing his edge, and inching ever closer to the Masters family plot in Greenmount Cemetery. He'd failed to anticipate the threat posed not only by Pill City but by a crop of ambitious imitators as well. In the weeks since the riots, at least five

copycat crews have begun selling opiates in Baltimore and
DC, also using encrypted smartphones and messaging apps to
traffic drugs. The region, it seems, has become an incubator
for high-tech criminal startups.

But Jimmy, ever the traditionalist, remains wedded to a
low-tech approach.

"We do things face-to-face, old school–like," he's fond of saying. But with 2016 beckoning, the younger men assembled here
know "old school" is no longer a viable business strategy, and
that Masters's aversion to technology makes him less relevant—
and more vulnerable—every day. Still, they listen politely to the
once-untouchable syndicate leader, knowing he has more experience in the game than all of them combined and would personally put a bullet through each of their heads if the need arose.

They've all heard the stories about Jimmy's temper: the in-
numerable murders carried out by him and his men, the tor-
turing of their enemies for information, the rumors he'd had
entire families killed for their patriarchs' transgressions. The
most chilling story they'd heard concerned a murder Jimmy
was said to have committed back in 2001. In November of that
year, the crime boss was eating breakfast with a 19-year-old
drug courier, a new hire for his organization, when the kid
started clicking away on his BlackBerry. Masters, cutting into
a spinach and American cheese omelet, implored the kid to
pay attention—he had some tricks of the trade he wanted
to pass along. Still, the keyboard tapper kept at it, until Jimmy
couldn't stand it anymore.

The next night, his new hire was found in an East Baltimore trash bin, a cheese-smeared knife lodged in his chest, a
crushed BlackBerry beside him. It was one of at least seven
murders Masters was rumored to have personally committed

over the years. So even in a room full of young, street-hardened gangsters, the old man commands a hard-won respect.

"In the corporate world, they got a word for what these fools are doing to our business . . . it's called disruption," says Masters, who's been reading *Wired* magazine in an effort to get a hold on Brick and Wax's capabilities. "But we still got some things they don't. We still got our experience, our organizations, and our connections. And when these trifling children are gone, we'll all still be here, making money."

With his proposal out in the open, Masters goes around the room, asking each gang leader for his thoughts. All seem amenable to his plan, with the exception of Tyson Ed. Barely 20 years old, Tyson Ed is one of the youngest gangsters in the room, and far more comfortable with technology than his host. Before Pill City's formation, Tyson Ed's gang had been the most technologically adept in Baltimore, using encrypted messaging on their iPhones to organize most of their re-ups.

"Respectfully, I've got to disagree with you on this, Jimmy," Tyson Ed says, his voice clear and steady, betraying no hint of nervousness. "I know these niggas been taking business from us, that they touched Stacks. But from everything we know, they good businessmen. Maybe the best thing to do is find a way to work with them, get a piece of that pie ourselves."

Tyson Ed must know that speaking out against Masters's plan is risky. He must have heard the stories about gangsters who'd opposed the old man in the past, only to end up dead. But Tyson Ed fancies himself a new kind of slinger, more attuned to Pill City's way of doing business than he's ever been to Masters's. If he doesn't stand up to the old man and his way of doing things, he's probably wondering, who here will?

"I think we should put out word to BGF, see whether they

willing to do business," Tyson Ed says. "There's money to be made for all of us."

Masters, trying hard to keep his temper in check, thanks Tyson Ed for his input. He asks his guests to reconvene three nights later and sends each home with a bottle of expensive cognac and cigars.

Less than 24 hours later, Tyson Ed is parking outside his parents' rowhome in Sandtown-Winchester—dropping by to deliver some fresh chicken from Lexington Market—when a gray Ford Explorer pulls up alongside his late-model Lexus.

He looks over and sees Mondo pointing a TEC-9 out of the driver's side window.

"Nah, yo," Tyson Ed says, just before a hollow-point round tears through his cheek. This reporter is stationed in a nearby vehicle, having just arrived for a scheduled interview with Tyson Ed, when the killing occurs. Mondo fires a few more rounds into the Lexus before fleeing, the gunfire so loud, it sets off car alarms across the neighborhood. The racket brings a number of residents out into the streets, Tyson Ed's mother, Erica Sperry, among them. She sees a bullet-riddled corpse in her son's Lexus, its face rendered unrecognizable by a series of gaping wounds. She tells herself it can't possibly be her "little boy." He'd called just a few minutes earlier to say he was dropping by with dinner, sounding calm as can be.

"It's not him," she tells the first police officer on scene. "No chance."

Only when the cops pull an ID from Tyson Ed's pocket does she allow herself to scream.

As crime scene technicians dig bullets out from the side of Tyson Ed's Lexus, Damage holds court several blocks east in

BGF's West Baltimore clubhouse, giving a handful of enforcers a pep talk.

"Who here ready to kill for the mothafucking cause?" the BGF field marshal says.

The gang's just received word from an informant that Jimmy Masters's younger brother, Ezekiel "Zeke" Masters, had recently arrived in Baltimore, summoned from Kansas City to help coordinate the organization's counteroffensive against Pill City. Also said to have flown in to help the family is Jimmy's only surviving son, Andrew "Blackrock" Masters, who handles his father's business interests in South Florida.

"This an opportunity for us," Damage tells his fellow gangsters. "We might not get them all in one spot like this again."

Damage, still irked by his waning influence in BGF, had quickly seized on news of Zeke and Blackrock's arrival, viewing it as an opportunity to both reassert his authority as field marshal and demonstrate his tactical prowess. Slim, he knows, is out of town for the weekend, overseeing a drug delivery to a BGF set in Cincinnati. As a result, Lyric had had little choice but to entrust Damage with the mission.

The Masters Organization, Damage tells his enforcers, are now aligned with three other gangs—the Gangster Disciples, Highlandtown Soldiers, and Bloods—in an effort to recapture their old corners. Only Purple City had declined an invitation to join their coalition.

"Jimmy bringing Zeke and Blackrock in means they fitting to come at us hard with them other crews," Damage says. "So we going to come at them first."

The enforcers nod in approval, several sliding fresh clips into their weapons. Some of Baltimore's most skilled killers are in this room tonight, including Lionel "Dome" Simmons, 22, an ex-con who's decked out in an Orioles jersey and expensive jeans, clothes he'd stripped off a Masters Organization corner boy he'd shot and critically wounded eight nights earlier; De-Shawn "Royal" Monroe, 25, who's toking on a blunt thick as a Rothschild cigar; and Train Lockwood, who frequently serves as a getaway driver for BGF's assassination missions.

Damage is thinking he's assembled the perfect crew for to-night's outing, until the clubhouse door swings open.

"Oh, *hell* no, I know y'all wasn't trying to get down without me," Slim says, strutting into the room wearing a pair of cam-ouflage pants, a new gold Rolex gleaming on his wrist.

"Welcome back, nigga," says Train, standing up to embrace Slim. The other gangsters—all except Damage—whoop and holler at the return of BGF's most prolific killer, just back from Cincinnati.

"Let's mount up," Slim says, bumping fists with everyone but the field marshal. "Time to take it to these niggas."

They drive toward Jimmy's gambling den in Train's Yukon, Slim in the front seat, Royal, Dome, and Damage in back. Slim, having removed his shirt to show off his new BGF tattoos, is caressing the barrel of his prized possession: a glistening, .45-caliber revolver inlaid with ivory and white gold, a gun so rare and valuable, he rarely removes it from its storage box.

"Nice piece, ain't it?" he asks Train.

"Yeah, that shit's tight, son. Where'd you get it?"

Slim explains that he'd taken the gun from a "dead terror-ist" during the Iraq War, a man he'd riddled with bullets in front of his wife and son.

"The nigga I got it from, Crazy Kasim, he was a militia member."

"A what?"

"A militia member," says Slim. "A murdering-ass nigga who don't give a fuck. They got militias, same way we got gangs. Only they clique up by ethnicity, heritage. Everything over there all ancient and shit."

"Why they call him crazy?" asks Train.

"Because he did the wildest shit," says Slim. "I mean, this nigga would just roll up on a patrol [of U.S. troops] in his truck and empty a clip on them. Killed a couple niggas I knew, so you *know* I wanted to get his ass."

He continues: "But it took mad long, because we couldn't find his ass at first. His militia . . . they had all these safe houses, kind of like we got. But one day we found out he was holed up in this regular house, his uncle's house in Fallujah, visiting with his family. It was his uncle's birthday or some shit."

"How'd you find out where he at?" says Dome.

"Man, we had spies *all* over that country, people helping us out for a little cash," Slim says. "Just like we got here."

"Word?"

"Hell, yeah. Niggas be snitching like crazy in Iraq, but they usually get popped for it later on, same as here."

"Damn," says Train, who's driving slowly now, wanting to hear the rest of the story before they reach Jimmy's spot.

"So we roll up to Kasim's uncle's house," Slim continues, "jump out, run up on the door before anybody inside got a chance to get ready. First room we bust into, I see that nigga Kasim standing in the corner, people all around him. His family, they laughing and eating desserts and shit. So we like, aight, everybody get your hands up. And everybody do it but Kasim, who I'm watching real close like, because I *know* he crazy. And sure enough, that nigga reaches behind his back and comes out with this here whistle [gun], draws it so fast he almost lights all of us up.

"But one of our people squeezes off first. Then I squeeze off. And Kasim . . . Kasim got torn up for real, straight blasted like I ain't never seen."

"So what his people do?" Train says.

"Nothing they could do. They just stood there, crying, begging us not to shoot them. Blood and brains was all over them, their food, the walls, ceiling. Kasim's wife was holding this little boy, Kasim's son, I think, and they had, like, little pieces of him splashed on their shirts and faces."

"Shit was fierce," says Dome.

"Always," Slim says, easing the gun back into his waistband.

"You ever use it?" Train asks, nodding at the glistening pistol.

"Not even once."

"Why tonight?"

"'Cause it's Zeke," says Slim. "He a legend. If that nigga going to die by my hand, he deserve my best."

"Brother's Keeper"

Niggas act like they never even heard of the code.

—ZEKE MASTERS

June 2015, Ellwood Park, Baltimore

Detective Grayson and his sergeant, Mike Malinowski, are speeding through Ellwood Park just after 10:30 p.m., trying to get to Jimmy's casino before the "fireworks start," Grayson says. He's just received a text from his informant, Derek Curry, saying he'd spotted Zeke and Blackrock Masters inching through the drive-thru line at Long John Silver's, smoking blunts in a BMW with out-of-state plates.

"If those two fools are in Baltimore, that can pretty much only mean one thing," says Grayson. "Somebody's getting ready to bust shots."

The Long John Silver's is a block and a half from Jimmy's gambling den, the investigators know, having raided the casino several times over the years. Each time they'd shut it down, Jimmy would find a new front man to reopen it as a "social club," always under a different name. The current moniker is "Manny's," a tribute to Jimmy's deceased father, Emmanuel.

"Jimmy keeps changing the name, but it's the same bullshit going on inside—cards, numbers, dogfighting in the basement," says Malinowski. "The Masters Organization is pretty unsophisticated, especially compared with these new guys [Pill City], but unsophisticated can still make you a lot of money in this city."

Grayson guns a pair of red lights, but not before taking in the view to his left: The windowed towers of downtown Baltimore glimmering in the distance, lightened by a low-hanging moon.

"You know, it'd be nice to actually enjoy that view for a change, stop and smell the roses," he says.

"A drug cop in this town, enjoy himself?" says Malinowski. "Keep dreaming."

"I got three kings," says Zeke Masters, laying his winning hand on the card table.

"Goddamn, you are one lucky fool," Jimmy says, watching as his brother collects another pile of winnings. "Always catching your card on the river."

The other two players at the table, Blackrock and Mondo, are equally perturbed, shaking their heads at the sight of their shrinking chip piles.

"What can I say?" Zeke says, grinning. "Some of us just blessed."

"Yeah, well, I hope you brought enough blessings for everybody," Jimmy says. "Because we need some right about now."

Zeke, the number-two man in his brother's organization, arrived in Baltimore just this morning, summoned by Jimmy to help prosecute the war against Pill City—a conflict, Jimmy says, that will decide the fate of their family-operated drug syndicate and likely determine whether "we stay in business."

Zeke knows Jimmy isn't exaggerating, for he'd witnessed the syndicate's handiwork firsthand in Kansas City: the bullet-riddled bodies of rivals BGF dumped in the streets, the speed with which they'd penetrated new markets with the help of technology, and the disdain they'd shown for established drug gangs.

"Ain't no joke out there," Zeke says during a break between hands, the men refilling their cups of cognac. "Any way you look at it, we getting handled."

Just shy of his fifty-second birthday, Zeke has no illusions about the drug game. He's killed at least 18 people at his brother's behest between 1982 and 2015, he says, and "crippled" countless others with gunfire. Like Jimmy, Zeke is what modern-day gangsters call an "old boy" or "old head," terms reserved for seasoned hustlers in their 50s and 60s, guys who've spent their entire lives in the game.

"I might be an old-ass dinosaur," Zeke likes to say, pointing to the various handguns concealed beneath his clothes, "but I still got my claws."

Balding, overweight, and suffering from sickle cell anemia, Zeke bears little resemblance to the muscle-bound, 27-year-old enforcer who, in the spring of 1991, secured his place in urban underworld history by assassinating both Jameis "House" Joseph and his son, Bobby Joseph, Baltimore's leading heroin dealers at the time.

The killings reshuffled Baltimore's underworld order near the tail end of the crack era, making Jimmy the undisputed king of the city's heroin markets. Zeke, too, saw his legend cemented by the killings, becoming one of the most feared enforcers in the country. With the Josephs eliminated, Jimmy

was able to cut a deal with House's suppliers, the Carranza
brothers, to import high-quality heroin from Mexico—a deal
that made the Masters Organization Baltimore's largest opiate distributors.

That was 25 years ago, Zeke knows, but Jimmy still believes
his little brother can "pull off a miracle" like he did against the
Josephs in 1991: that he can swoop into Baltimore for a week
and, with a few, well-planned assassinations, reverse all of Pill
City's gains.

But it's not the 1990s anymore, Zeke says, and Pill City is
no House Joseph.

"Ain't no putting this genie back in the bottle," he tells the
men at the card table. "These Pill City boys playing a different game than anybody we done battled. Niggas act like they
never even heard of the code."

"The code," these gangsters know, is an unwritten set of
rules for the urban underworld, a set of protocols by which
criminals conduct their affairs—or *did* conduct them, before
Pill City came along. The code allows for killings of all kinds,
so long as they meet certain criteria: (1) an upstart crew doesn't
go to war with an established one without first pursuing ne-
gotiations; (2) syndicate leaders like Brick and Wax don't mask
their true identities from rivals. That way, crime bosses can
be held accountable for their organization's actions. Last, the
code bars the targeting of civilians: men, women, and children
with no involvement in the game.

Pill City, Zeke says, has violated, or showed contempt for,
all three.

"And they *still* getting more customers every day, more territory, too," Jimmy says.

Indeed, despite Jimmy's multigang alliance, BGF is killing
or wounding between six and eight enemy gangsters around

the country for every one casualty they themselves suffer. At that rate, Jimmy says, the war with his organization could be lost by fall, if not sooner.

"How do we fix this?" he asks Zeke.

"Shit, I've been asking myself that same question."

Back in Kansas City, Zeke explains, the family's operations are in as much disarray as they are in Baltimore, with BGF crews gaining more market share—and murdering more rival dealers—every week. Things are so bad, Zeke says, he wants to return to Missouri and get his "own house in order." But Jimmy tells him Baltimore's the priority.

"If we fall here, everything else falls, too."

Zeke arches his eyebrows, his way of registering dissent with his brother. As he does, Jimmy realizes how much Zeke looks like their father—the same strong chin, the same penetrating eyes, his body visibly worn down by the demands of their business, just like their dad in his final days. Jimmy recalls a Halloween they'd celebrated long ago, when Zeke was six, maybe seven years old; remembers how happy he'd been to sit on their father's lap, wearing the Superman costume their mother had stitched for him.

"I'm Soup-a-man!" Zeke announced, though at the time, their father was the one who seemed made of steel.

Emmanuel Masters had been critically wounded by one of House Joseph's enforcers several weeks before Halloween—a shooting that left Baltimore's underworld holding its collective breath. No one knew whether the elder Masters would survive the five shots to his torso, chest, and legs, or, if he did, whether he'd be the same fearsome gangster who, in the span of five years, had turned a single dope corner on North Paca Street into a multimillion-dollar drug trafficking operation. Watching his father limp through their front door Halloween night, just released from the hospital with bullets still lodged his body, Jimmy was prouder of his dad than he'd ever been.

"Promise me one thing," Emmanuel told Jimmy before heading to church the next day.

The wounded kingpin had found religion while convalescing, and would attend Sunday services for the rest of his life.

"Anything, Dad," Jimmy said.

"Promise me you'll keep Zeke out of all this."

Jimmy nodded his assent, already aware of his father's plan for Zeke: attend college, get a "legitimate" job, and steer clear of the family business, "so that not everyone with the name Masters ends up a gangster," Emmanuel once said.

Jimmy, in contrast, wanted nothing more than to follow in his father's footsteps. He'd even dropped out of school to sell drugs for the syndicate full time.

"Zeke won't be involved in none of this," Jimmy promised his father. "My word on that."

"Your word's all I need," said Emmanuel. "You're your brother's keeper. Never forget that."

"I won't, Dad."

Emmanuel would live another nine years, time he'd spend grooming Jimmy to take over the syndicate, while Zeke focused on academics and athletics. The teen's size, strength, and intelligence on the football field were so impressive, his coach, Lawrence "Larry" Booker, named him starting linebacker for the varsity squad his sophomore year.

"I'm very, very proud of you," Emmanuel told his son in the fall of 1980, after Zeke brought home a report card full of As. "Can't wait to see what you accomplish next year."

But Emmanuel didn't make it that far.

In the last week of October, two Joseph family enforcers sprayed Emmanuel's cream-colored Cadillac Eldorado with automatic gunfire. Police found the crime boss slumped over the steering wheel, a Christian music station playing on the radio.

Zeke learned of his father's death in the middle of football practice. With tears streaming down his cheeks, the young man took a knee on the sideline, said a short prayer, and then, without a word of complaint, returned to the field to finish the afternoon drills.

"That's a man right there," Booker told his assistant coaches as they watched the scene unfold. "He'll be somebody if he gets the chance."

Jimmy, reeling from their father's death, had other ideas.

Believing the syndicate vulnerable to further attacks, he decided his brother would have to drop everything to help him protect the family's interests. In his first act as kingpin, he ordered Zeke to quit school and come work for the family.

"Why are you doing this?" Zeke asked. He'd planned to attend the University of Maryland, earn a business degree, and open a restaurant downtown—a venture his father had promised to bankroll.

"Because it's the best thing for the family," Jimmy said. "With Dad gone, it's my job to use every asset at my disposal to defend what's ours."

Zeke's size, intelligence, and physical strength—attributes prized as much on drug corners as on the football field—were things Jimmy refused to "give away for nothing," he told his brother, "especially now that the Josephs are making moves against us again."

"Besides," he added, "this is what Dad told me he wanted."

Zeke, who would have done anything for their father, took Jimmy at his word. He'd soon become one of the most prodigious gangland killers in America, leading exactly the kind of life Emmanuel had hoped he'd avoid.

And all these years later, Jimmy still hasn't told him the truth.

Now, as Zeke deals another hand of poker, Jimmy wonders if it was all worth it: the killings, the deceit, the loss of so many friends and loved ones, their father among them. Might he have been better served to honor his promise, to have actually been his brother's keeper and spared him from this life of crime?

He's pondering this question when a deafening burst of gunfire rings out in the street. As he's done so many times over the years, Jimmy tells his little brother to "go handle it," and Zeke, ever the loyal soldier, rises from his chair. He takes a long look back at Jimmy before exiting, looking so much like their father did back in the day—tired, sorrowful, but strong—it gives Jimmy chills.

"Wait," Jimmy calls out, sensing, perhaps, what awaits Zeke outside.

But the aging enforcer is already out the door. Right away, he sees two of the family's security men lying wounded in the street, writhing in pain. Standing around them are four BGF members—Slim, Dome, Damage, and Train—Slim clutching a still-smoking ivory and gold pistol.

"Should've stayed in KC, nigga," Slim says, pointing the gun at Zeke.

Jimmy is fleeing down a back alley when the fatal shot rings out.

Later that night, the kingpin kneels to pray for forgiveness but can't find the words.

Grayson and Malinowski arrive 10 minutes too late.

"We should've been here," Grayson says, looking down at Zeke's corpse. "We had the tip."

"You can't think that way," Malinowski says. "We got here soon as we could. You were blowing through every red."

"Yeah, hell of a lot of good it did."

Grayson is tired of all the killing—the corpses that keep piling up thanks to Pill City's ruthless, methodical approach. Tyson Ed and Zeke are just the latest casualties in the ongoing Opiate Wars, Grayson says, with more bodies surely on the way. He knows the arrest of Pill City's leaders would severely disrupt the syndicate's operations, slowing the record pace of homicides and nonfatal shootings in Baltimore and elsewhere. But after roughly three months of painstaking, costly investigation, the Baltimore Police, DEA, and FBI have made little progress in the drug looting probe.

All their work—the grueling interrogations, the mind-numbing surveillance, the long nights spent poring over case files—have gotten investigators "nowhere," Grayson says. To date, he and Malinowski have interviewed more than two dozen BGF members, some of the gangsters charged with crimes ranging from drug possession and distribution to gang assault and weapons offenses. Yet not one of them has disclosed information about Brick or Wax, all insisting they know nothing about the kingpins.

"Who these guys are, their actual IDs . . . that's the holy grail for us," Grayson says while canvassing for witnesses near Jimmy's casino. "Right now, we just don't know."

Meanwhile, Pill City customers continue to die at a shocking pace. Today alone, at least seven more drug users have fatally overdosed on stolen opiates trafficked from Baltimore, the addicts dying in St. Louis, Newark, and Milwaukee. That's three fewer overdose deaths than the day before, when at least five men, three women, and two teenagers lost their lives to Pill City product across the country.

By year's end, the number of fatal overdose victims believed felled by Pill City opiates will surpass 400—the most
deaths linked to an inner-city drug gang in a single year since
the crack epidemic, authorities say. The regional breakdowns
show the scope of BGF's reach: 32 users dead from syndicate-
supplied opiates in the Baltimore/DC area; 20 in Detroit; 19 in
Memphis; 23 in Milwaukee; 40 in Philadelphia; 19 in Cincinnati; 36 in Atlanta; 74 in South Florida; 50 in St. Louis; 44 in Kansas City; and 36 and 38, respectively, in Camden and Newark.*

More than 230 other users have survived overdoses from
Pill City opiates, many resuscitated by syndicate slingers
themselves. Per Lyric's suggestion, BGF sets across the country have begun carrying doses of Narcan, the nasal spray ver-
sion of naloxone, which can revive a dying user when sprayed
up his or her nose.

"These guys are literally trying to keep their customers
alive so they can keep making money off them," Grayson tells
his sergeant as they head back to the Western District station.
"And they're *still* dropping like flies."

Hopping on the interstate a little later, Grayson decides he
needs a break from "all this ugliness." He thinks of Patti Sinclair; remembers how pretty she'd looked that morning in her
father's pharmacy, how helpful she'd been with that surveillance video. The detective has been meaning to phone her
with an update on the drug looting probe and a request that
they grab dinner. But he's been so busy working the Pill City
case, he keeps forgetting to call. It's what his ex-wife Lisa once
dismissively referred to as "detective's amnesia," shortly before she moved out.

---

* Totals are based on author's examination of death records in these cities
 and their suburbs as well as interviews with law enforcement officials,
 drug dealers, overdose survivors, and families of overdose victims.

Now the detective locates Patti's number in his phone, gets up his nerve, and dials.

She answers on the fifth ring, her voice strangely giddy.

"Detective Jamaaaaaal, I thought you'd never call."

Grayson's surprised by how loopy she sounds, a stark contrast to the calm, serious woman he'd met at Fred's Discount back in May.

"How are you, Patti? Great to hear your voice again."

"It's great to hear *you* again, Detective," Patti says, her words slightly slurred.

Grayson figures she's probably thrown back a few too many beers, maybe smoked a little weed. Nothing Grayson himself hasn't done before to deal with stress.

"I just wanted to check in, see how you and your dad are doing," he says. "Sounds like you're doing *real* well."

"Yeah, I'm OK. Better now that you called," Patti says, giggling.

"You partying tonight?"

"Nah, nothing major," Patti says. "Just took a couple of Roxys. I've got some more, if you're interested."

"Roxys, as in Roxicodone?"

"Yeah."

"You got a scrip for them?"

Patti's silence is all the answer he needs.

"I guess it's none of my business," Grayson says.

"It certainly isn't, Detective," says Patti. "But I'll tell you what. You bring your nosy ass over to my place tonight, along with a bottle of wine. *Maybe* I'll forgive you."

"You serious, girl?"

"You know I am."

Grayson would love to spend an evening with Patti—he hasn't been with anyone since his divorce—but somehow, tonight doesn't feel right. Not while Patti's high on painkillers and clearly not herself.

He begs off, explaining his concerns, and Patti thanks him for his honesty.

"I feel like an idiot," she says. "But thank you for being a gentleman. Truth be told, I'm probably taking too many [pills] lately."

"How many we talking?"

"Hmmm, maybe 10, 12 a day?"

The irony of a pharmacist's daughter getting high on Roxicodone isn't lost on her, Patti says, especially since she'd been weighing whether to take the police department's entrance exam.

"After that day with you in my dad's store, I realized I might make a pretty good cop," she says. "So that's all the more reason to get cleaned up."

She'd been in rehab twice before for prescription opiate abuse, she says, and thought she'd had her addiction beat.

"I hadn't touched a pill in months, but those delivery guys started bringing them right to people's doors . . . I don't know why, but I gave in."

Grayson is troubled by the revelation but not surprised. BGF's penetration of inner-city drug markets has been so rapid, it makes sense a recovering user would have found her way back to painkillers through its delivery service.

"My plan is to get a bed date soon as I can," Patti says, using a slang term for the day on which one enters rehab. "Maybe when I'm done, we can get together?"

For a moment, Grayson thinks he ought to just drive to her place, and throw caution to the wind. Then he imagines the potential trial against Pill City's founders—Patti or her dad's testimony discredited by the fact that she'd had a relationship with a detective probing the very syndicate that supplied her with drugs.

No way he's going to jeopardize months of work for a romantic tryst, he thinks.

"Be safe, Patti," he tells her, trying not to sound too cold. "I'll keep you posted on where we're at with the case."

They tell each other good night, with Grayson pulling up outside the station just as the line goes dead.

The next time he hears Patti's name, it's from Fred Sinclair, calling to invite him to his daughter's funeral.

"Expansion"

We have another export that is . . . quite good.

—Philippe Carranza

His first night in the new apartment, Brick wakes up screaming.

"Goddamn," the drug lord shouts into the dark, eyes darting around his bedroom.

He half expects to find Arthur Kane lurking by the door, but once he gets his bearings, he realizes there's no one there—just the new dresser and entertainment center he'd had delivered last week. The apartment is modern and sleek, a spacious one-bedroom in Baltimore County. Wax, too, recently rented a new crib, his directly across the street from his business partner's. With drug profits rolling in, the boys thought it best to move out of Gilmor, especially since Wax's mom, Brenda Harris, is trying to get clean and, her son says, doesn't need a pair of drug kingpins living under her roof. (Brenda's still in the dark about the boys' involvement in the game. As far as she knows, they're excelling in school and running some kind of "computer business" on the side.)

Moving out of the apartment he'd shared with Wax and Brenda since 2008 has been difficult for Brick, he says. Over the past year, he's begun exhibiting textbook symptoms of bipolar disorder, and he's certain he has inherited the illness from his mother. Living on his own seems only to have made things worse: Brick's depressed, lethargic, paranoid, and anxious some weeks, but at other times, he feels overjoyed and filled with energy, "like a god, like I'm untouchable," he says.

"I've been uneven, highs and lows," he explains, "steep slopes, like my mom used to have."

Brick knows he should see a doctor right away but admits he doesn't want to lose what he calls the "positive" elements of the disease: creativity, confidence, boundless energy, an increased appetite for risks. After all, such traits, applied properly, can be useful in his line of work.

"It feels good when I'm on the good side of it," Brick says of his illness. "I kind of don't want to lose that."

Now, as the first sliver of sun peeks through his bedroom window, Brick shakes the nightmare about Arthur from his mind and lets the "good feeling" come again, hoping to make it last as long as possible.

Because "when the bad comes," he says, "I'm not myself."

That evening, Damage gets his nightly check-in call from Brick at 9 p.m. sharp, the teenager's voice oozing confidence. Pill City's rise has molded him into a man, Damage thinks, a far cry from the sad, defeated-looking child he used to see shuffling out of Arthur Kane's apartment each morning before school.

"What's the word, D?" Brick says, sounding hyped, like he's just downed five cups of coffee. "We good?"

"Yeah, everything lookin' smooth," Damage says.

"No eyes on us tonight?"

"Nah, we checked the whole neighborhood . . . roofs, vacants, cars, everything. No DEA, no police, none of Jimmy's people, nobody."

Later, they discuss the war with Jimmy's syndicate, both agreeing it seems to have been won, with the old man rumored to have fled to South America after Zeke's murder.

"If we just about done with those niggas," Brick says, "I think it's time we make that other move, with the raw."

Brick's already ordered tens of thousands more pills from Agora Marketplace, the Dark Web pharmacy that's been selling Pill City drugs to round out their looted inventory—supplies of which have been dwindling by the day. He's also convinced BGF to begin producing pills containing fentanyl—the opiate painkiller that can be 100 times more powerful than morphine—using equipment and chemicals the syndicate procured online. Distribution of those drugs have helped cause a nationwide spike in fentanyl-related deaths. Now, he says he wants to "get deeper" into the heroin game, too, by "getting some type of regular connect for Mexican product." Given his existing connections, Brick says, might Damage be willing to arrange for a meeting with his "Mexican friends"?

"Cuz, I thought you'd never ask," Damage says, still eager to prove his value to his BGF brethren, especially after Slim's hijacking of the casino mission outside Jimmy's. "We about due for an expansion."

Four nights later, in a small, upscale restaurant not far from DC, Damage sits down at a table with one of the region's biggest heroin suppliers, Philippe Carranza, 57, and his translator, Rafael Alvarez. The three men order lobsters, washing them down with expensive wine. It's Damage's first time meeting the Mexican drug trafficker, and he's as dapper as advertised, decked out in a Gucci suit and Ralph Lauren Black Label tie.

"The seafood back home is better," Carranza says in Spanish, Alvarez dutifully translating for his boss. "We have another export that is . . . quite good."

"Better than good, from what I hear," Damage says. "The best."

The restaurant is empty except for the kitchen staff and a single waiter, Carranza's people having called ahead to have the place closed for a "private meeting." It's a prime example of the kind of power he wields on the East Coast, where Carranza's Mexican friends call him "El Santo," or the saint, because of his famously boundless generosity, but certain enemies know him as "El Diablo," the devil, because of his equally stunning capacity for cruelty. Case in point: He's said to have once ordered a rival trafficker choked to death with his own severed testicles. He's rumored twice to have had men bludgeoned to death because they did not pay their drug debts. On at least two other occasions, he's believed to have personally executed treasonous underlings, blowing their limbs off one at a time with a shotgun, starting with their legs.

Carranza runs his trafficking business with his older brother, Francisco, 62, known to friends and enemies alike as "El Forzudo," the strongman, because of his seemingly ageless physique and obsession with fitness. Their operation serves as a subsidiary of the Sinaloa Cartel, the world's largest, richest drug-dealing organization, which is headed by the notorious drug lord Joaquin "El Chapo" Guzman, currently imprisoned in Ciudad Juarez.

Damage, who had arranged tonight's meeting through a Sinaloa-connected BGF franchise in Chicago, tells Carranza the price Pill City is willing to pay for Sinaloa heroin—a number well into the millions.

"I like your idea very much, as will Francisco," Carranza says of his brother. "There is, of course, the problem of our mutual friend."

That "mutual friend," Damage knows, is Jimmy Masters, to whom the Carranzas have been selling heroin ever since Zeke assassinated House Joseph in 1991. The relationship between the Carranzas and Jimmy's syndicate historically has been a friendly one, with the Masters family paying for drug shipments on time and the Carranzas staying out of Jimmy's affairs. But lately, Jimmy's people have been asking for extensions on their payments, even requesting that the Carranzas lower their prices.

"You and your people have put him under tremendous pressure," Carranza tells Damage. "I know he's on the run. But he's still upright."

"Ain't like we not trying to find him."

"Of course," Carranza says. "But for us to do business in a way that's mutually beneficial, we feel you must . . . supplant him indefinitely. Sometime in the near future."

"I think we can make that happen," says Damage.

"Then we have a deal," Carranza says.

The traffickers shake hands, clink glasses, and call for another bottle of wine.

PART III

THE FALLEN

"They Changed the Game"

It's like a double life.

—Brick

After being cooped up writing code for more than three months, Brick and Wax decide to go out and celebrate Pill City's deal with the Carranzas—not at a strip club or bar, but at one of Baltimore's nerdiest hangout spots: the Ultrazone Laser Tag and Family Video Arcade in Eastpoint Mall.

"Ow, you got me!" Wax shouts, clutching his chest as Brick blasts him with a harmless laser beam.

"Man, you're too slow!" Brick says, laughing loudly, in the midst of another manic episode. "We need to send your ass to boot camp or something."

The business partners have hardly stepped outdoors since the riots—coding for long stretches most every day and night—but there's no disputing their work has made them rich. Since April 27, Brick and Wax have earned a shared total of over $5 million, their cut of an approximately $29 million pool of earnings collected by BGF franchises around the country, plus Dark Web drug sales. Thanks to encryption, Pill City is selling opiates in dozens of America's most economically distressed, racially segregated communities and beyond.

"To our dreams coming true," a jubilant Brick says in the mall's food court, clinking his cup of Mountain Dew against Wax's Pepsi bottle. Watching the boys swig soft drinks and munch on pizza, it's unlikely any mall-goer would guess that they are drug kingpins complicit in a wave of deaths across the country. Watching them crack jokes and ogle girls, few would suspect that, at this very moment, they're carrying loaded Sig Sauer 38s in their waistbands, the bulge of their firearms hidden by freshly starched, button-down polos.

"It's like a double life," Brick is fond of saying of the boys' private and public personas. "Like being two people in one."

He had demonstrated that duality four nights earlier, when Damage took him and Wax to visit a deadbeat customer in East Baltimore. The trip was made at the behest of Lyric and several other BGF franchise leaders, who, despite the money Brick and Wax were helping them earn, remained concerned the teens were "too soft, too clean." They feared the boys might snitch if subjected to police interrogations. To allay these concerns, the various franchise heads proposed that the coders "get their hands dirty."

So, with the teens at his side, Damage had burst through the deadbeat addict's back door, past his screaming wife, and into the bathroom where Isaiah "Zey" Walker—an out-of-work plumber who owed Pill City nearly $7,000 in accumulated drug debts—stood naked in front of the sink, shaving his week-old stubble.

"What the fuck?" Zey yelled just as Brick opened fire, lighting up the bathroom like the Fourth of July.

When the smoke cleared, Zey lay dead in a puddle of shaving cream and blood, his face and chest riddled with bullet holes. As his wife came running toward the bathroom, screaming her husband's name, Brick put two rounds through her chest, too.

"Bitch loud as hell," Brick said as Victoria Walker fell to the floor.

On the drive home, Damage praised his cousin for his "good shooting" back at Zey's, proud of how far he'd come since April.

"You learn quick," he said, looking in his rearview mirror to find Brick beaming.

Wax, in contrast, seemed rattled by the killings, his hands still shaking 15 minutes after they'd fled. He felt guilty about his involvement in the attack, believing the shooting of Zey's wife especially needless. But he kept these thoughts to himself, not wanting to seem "too soft, too clean," as BGF's leaders suspected.

Tonight, scarfing pizza at Ultrazone, he's feeling a little better, happy to be playing games like a "normal kid," he says, instead of organizing drug sales and helping commit murders. And yet something still feels off to Wax. Part of it is his guilt about Zey and Victoria Walker; unlike Brick, Wax had never taken part in a murder before, and he found the experience horrifying.

But more than that, he's worried about his best friend.

Brick's "been acting real strange," Wax says when Brick steps away to use the bathroom. Over the past few months, he's either been "depressed real bad, or all happy, full of energy."

Just like Renata Feeney, Wax thinks.

Now, as the boys prepare for another game of laser tag, Wax asks Brick whether he feels OK.

"Never felt better," he says, pointing the laser gun at his friend.

The flight from Colombia to DC is so bumpy, Jimmy vomits twice.

"Miss, can I trouble you for another glass of water?" he asks the flight attendant in first class.

"Of course, sir," she says, bringing Jimmy not just his drink but another paper bag, too. She hovers near his seat for a few moments, cleaning a speck of food off his chin, tending to him as if he were a baby. "You poor thing, just hit the button if you need anything else."

Jimmy knows he's crossed some kind of threshold—that he's no longer a man who is feared but rather one who is pitied. Having recently turned 69, the gangster is in obvious decline: his bones hurting more each day, his loss of vision and hearing accelerating. Gone is the imposing, nattily dressed crime boss of old, replaced by a stoop-shouldered senior citizen in a sweatsuit.

But it's not just bad health that's bothering Jimmy; it's his conscience, too. He feels wholly responsible for Zeke's death, believing he'd deceived his brother in an unforgiveable way. He'd failed their father, too, ignoring his imploration to be his brother's keeper. Now his entire syndicate seems on the verge of collapse, and Jimmy is flying home empty-handed after failing to negotiate a heroin purchase with a prospective supplier—a rival of the Sinaloa Cartel—in South America. The trip became necessary after the Carranza brothers ditched Jimmy's syndicate in favor of Pill City.

"I'm obsolete," Jimmy tells Mondo and Blackrock when they pick him up at Dulles International Airport that night.

On the drive home, the crime boss finally acknowledges

that his low-tech approach is no longer viable—not at a time when iPhones, encryption, and the Dark Web are revolutionizing the way drugs are sold. He understands and accepts this reality; that's why he's making Blackrock acting head of the family, he says, and designating Mondo his second in command.

"You sure, Pop?" Blackrock says, clutching his father's hand, shocked by how much he's deteriorated in the weeks since Zeke's death.

"Sure as I'll ever be," says Jimmy, explaining that he'd failed to secure a new seller during his trip. "It's going to be up to you all to find a new connect."

"Don't worry," Blackrock says. "We'll find a way."

Halfway to Baltimore, he reminds his father to keep a low profile back home, since BGF's enforcers still want him dead. The family is throwing a birthday party next month for Blackrock's soon-to-be eight-year-old daughter, Patience, but neither he nor Mondo thinks Jimmy should attend.

"It's a risk, having you there," Mondo says. "Somebody could snitch to BGF."

"Let them snitch, then," Jimmy says. "I ain't going to cower no more. And I ain't missing my grandchild's birthday."

At Jimmy's house, they help him unpack and make dinner, then they all sit down to watch the evening news. A reporter covering the Freddie Gray case says that, more than three months after the riots, nearly all the criminals involved in the pharmacy lootings remain at large.

"I got to hand it to them niggas," Jimmy says of Brick, Wax, and their BGF brethren, marveling at the havoc they'd visited upon Baltimore—and his own family—since April. "They changed the game."

"Freelancers"

I would have never, ever, been able to get a legal job that pays this much.

—MALIK "SHILO" ROSS

The Carranzas' new heroin shipment is the bomb, Lyric says, their Mexican dope so popular with customers, "we had to order twice as much for next month."

"All our franchises are bringing new people on because of the amount of demand out there," says Lyric. "We need workers, niggas willing to put in the time. It's a 24/7 job right now."

Despite the risks of death or imprisonment, there's no shortage of young men clamoring to land jobs with Pill City: teens and 20-somethings looking to support their families, take out girls, or just make a little sneaker money. To increase daily productivity—and replace dead or jailed associates—BGF franchises are hiring four or five new delivery men a week, Lyric says, with some dealers even defecting from other crews to join the encrypted syndicate.

While their backgrounds vary, most BGF "freelancers," as Lyric calls them, share some common traits: Born and raised in impoverished inner-city neighborhoods, they have at least one parent who's been in prison or addicted to drugs; most have served time for drug offenses; and most consider drug dealing the only viable way to make a living wage in their neighborhoods.

"There's no opportunity in this city for people like me," says Malik "Shilo" Ross, 19, a newly hired BGF delivery man whose coverage zone spans five blocks in Cincinnati's Over-the-Rhine neighborhood. "I went to work for [Pill City] because they offer the best pay out of all the crews here. Ain't no legitimate business going to pay me that kind of money. And I got to have money, one way or another."

Shilo's journey from student to drug delivery man is typical among Pill City's freelance associates. He'd dropped out of high school halfway through his junior year, landing his position the way every non-BGF member does: by seeking out the local set leader, laying out his qualifications, and pleading for work.

"I was scrambling to make a few dollars any way I could, working the kitchen [in a] diner, going to school when I could," says Shilo, a handsome, confident kid with a history of convictions for marijuana and crack possession. "My record means I can't get the kind of job I want, but I got a baby daughter, so I've got to make enough to take care of her and her mom . . . something to buy them food and clothes with. The diner paid me minimum wage. That ain't enough after taxes to do nothing with. So I left that job, but not to slinging, not at first."

Shilo switched to a cook's job at Popeye's, which paid him a dollar more an hour. The restaurant had only afternoon hours available, so he stopped attending school in order to keep his position. The teen still wanted to earn his high school diploma, though, and figured he'd make up his lost credits over the summer.

But not long after taking the Popeye's job, Shilo's baby daughter contracted a rare bacterial infection. Her medical bills soared, and her dad worked as many shifts as possible to cover them.

"My daughter's mom was in the hospital with her around the clock, so I had to do my part," says Shilo. "We were sitting in her [hospital] room one night, looking at our baby, talking about the bills, and we was like 'What are we going to do?' Next day, I went down to talk to Oz [a BGF leader in Cincinnati]. He gave me an iPhone, some pills, some raw, put me to work right away."

Since then, Shilo has earned $200 a day from BGF, plus a $30 daily stipend for gas and food—better wages and perks than most legal jobs for men his age and color in Cincinnati. Indeed, young men selling drugs for Pill City and their high-tech imitators are earning far more than their predecessors, reversing decades of blatant exploitation by crew leaders and kingpins.

"I feel bad for the hustlers who came before us," Shilo says. "We can actually live on what they pay us. Those [dealers] couldn't."

Formerly, leaders of successful inner-city drug crews might earn several hundred thousand dollars annually, but they paid most of their employees $5 to $10 an hour. Pill City, as the group has done with so many other facets of the drug game, "disrupted" that norm, according to Calvacca, the Chicago narcotics detective, who has seen wages surge for street dealers in his city.

"It's incentivized dealing in a way we hadn't necessarily seen before," Calvacca says. "And that's brought more young men into the game."

Michael "Rabbit" Clements, a former Crips member who supervised half a dozen drug corners in New Orleans between 2007 and 2010, says the shift toward higher wages seems to have transformed inner-city opiate dealing in many communities.

"The system's always been unfair to them boys on the corners," says Clements, 31. "In my prime, I was making good money, about 200 Gs [annually], but the niggas who worked for me? They ain't make shit. Not that I didn't want to pay them better. I *did* want to. But every dollar that goes to them is one less dollar I can put toward my [heroin] package, and those dollars add up. So paying your people more means buying a weaker package, which means there's going to be fewer customers, which means you're making less money than before and your business is suffering. It's the same reason businessmen don't like it when the government raise the minimum wage. It hurts their bottom line. Well, slinging's the same way. Either I'm getting my dough and my corner boys get a little piece, or ain't *nobody* getting paid. Period."

That dynamic changed once Pill City launched its operations, Clements says. Because the tech-savvy syndicate built its business around looted and stolen opiates, its "product cost, their expenditures on drugs, was zero, so that freed them up to pass those savings on to their customers and employees," he says. "That's a situation that's basically unheard of if you a hustler, but [BGF] crews were able to do it because of the riots, because they stole all this prime product. And they had a lot of niggas hungry to come work for them."

Dane "Dink" Davis, a member of the Bloods in Los Angeles and supervisor of four once-bustling drug corners in that city, agrees. He says the expansion of BGF's operations in L.A. has slashed his gang's profits by almost half in 2015.

"Their people get paid more, so they hustle up, get more customers," says Dane. "We can't compete with them niggas on price, wages, none of that shit. They taking food out of our people's mouths."

To a man, BGF's freelancers say they're grateful for the cash.

"I would have never, ever been able to get a legal job that pays this much," Shilo says. "It makes my life better, makes my daughter and her mom's lives better. Now she's getting the medicine she needs. I got us a decent apartment. Way I see it, it's a blessing, this opportunity I got from BGF.

"My daughter might not be here if I didn't get this job," he adds. "We wouldn't be eating if I didn't get this job. This job means everything to me, even though to the police, this job makes me the enemy. I'm aight with that, though, if it means taking care of my baby girl and her mom."

As for high school, Shilo says: "I probably won't go back. Money I'm getting now's too good."

"The MASH Unit"

Oxy, Vikes, Roxys . . . I call them the holy trinity of opiate addiction. And heroin? She's a god unto herself.

—Dr. Corinne Heschel

September 14, 2015, West Baltimore

"What did you take tonight, Travis?" Dr. Corrine Heschel asks her 43-year-old patient, Travis Brown, his eyelids fluttering as paramedics roll him through the emergency room.

He's been rushed here to R Adams Cowley Shock Trauma Center straight from Oxy Alley, where a police officer found him lying unconscious in the street. Moments ago, paramedics revived him with Narcan. It's at least the twelfth Narcan save of the night in Baltimore, and it's not even 8 p.m.

"Can you hear me?" Heschel asks her still-groggy patient.

Brown nods his head and points to his pocket, where Heschel finds a bottle filled to the brim with 80 milligram oxycodone pills. From the track marks on his arms, legs, and feet, it appears Brown's been injecting his opiates, like most of the addicts Heschel treats these days.

"Oxy, Vikes, Roxys . . . I call them the holy trinity of

opiate addiction," she says a little later, after Brown's been stabilized and given his own take-home supply of Narcan. "And heroin? She's a god unto herself."

In her decade-plus career as an emergency room physician, Heschel's treated hundreds of poor African Americans in the throes of opiate overdose. But never as many as this year, she says. Some show up dead on arrival from the glut of drugs in their bloodstream, while others are mere minutes away from flatlining. Dozens of additional patients are brought to her each week with life-threatening gunshot wounds, many of them young men involved in the local drug trade.

"If what's going on with these pills, with all this heroin . . . is a war," says Heschel, "then this is the MASH unit. We treat everybody: the dealers and the addicts, soldiers, civilians, all of them. You OD or catch a bullet, you come see us. We don't discriminate."

Heschel and her colleagues in the ER have saved more than 30 overdosing patients this month but lost 14 others who'd snorted, injected, or swallowed opiates. Rarely does the blue-eyed, 45-year-old brunette have time to rest during her shifts, and tonight's no different. Not long after she discharges Brown, two more patients come rolling in on gurneys—a couple Heschel immediately recognizes as Gary and Brianna Moore, from Cherry Hill.

Both are overdosing on opiates, the paramedics explain, with neither responding to Narcan. Heschel and her fellow physicians spend a half hour trying to restart Gary's and Brianna's hearts. But it's no use.

"Call it," Heschel says at 9:58 p.m. She takes a final look at Gary's lifeless body, tears in her eyes, then steps outside.

"I can't believe we lost them both," she says, trying to regain her composure before returning to work.

The Moores weren't just any patients, Heschel says. They were her friends.

The pair first showed up in the ER six months earlier, after Gary had snorted too much Vicodin and lost consciousness. Heschel resuscitated him and moved on to other patients, but before he left the hospital, the 53-year-old tracked her down and kissed her on her cheek.

"I can't thank you enough," Gary said, explaining that he was a Maryland Transit Administration employee on the verge of retirement. Brianna, too, was a state-employed professional nearing the end of her career, as well as a pain pill addict. "We'd hate to miss out on those pensions," Gary said with a wink as they left the hospital. "So we got to get better."

Heschel's treated dozens of addicts who, despite their best efforts, never managed to recover. But Gary and Brianna seemed different, she says. They had two kids in college and a third serving in the U.S. Navy. Plus, the couple had "top-of-the-line" medical insurance through their government jobs. If anybody could beat their addictions, Heschel figured, it was them.

Standing outside the ER, she recalls the first time she'd laid eyes on Gary, his six-foot-two, 240-pound frame so large, the paramedics could barely lift him out of the ambulance.

"Here was this big, sweet, baldheaded man, million-dollar smile, and he couldn't stop using," Heschel recalls. "Brianna came with him in the ambulance. I told him what I tell everybody who's addicted to opiates: 'I'm going to give you this little bottle. It's a drug called Narcan. If you're OD'ing, somebody needs to spray it up one of your nostrils very quickly and you will *probably* be revived. I want you to carry it everywhere.' Well, Gary couldn't believe something like that existed. He said, 'So it's a miracle drug?' I said, 'Yeah, sort of, but don't count on it. Plenty of people get it too late and die.'"

Heschel gave Brianna her own Narcan supply, and the couple promised they'd take the drug everywhere they went. In the meantime, Heschel helped them both secure beds in an inpatient addiction treatment program. When they were deemed opiate free, the doctor took them out for a fancy dinner at Brianna's favorite restaurant in Baltimore's Little Italy.

"It was a celebration of life, of their lives," Heschel says.

She'd never befriended ER patients before—much less a married couple battling addiction—but Heschel felt the Moores needed "someone to believe in them." They'd kept their addiction a secret from their kids "out of shame," she says. And they weren't about to risk their government jobs by asking for support from colleagues.

"I wanted to help them during a difficult period in their lives, because they needed a friend, and I wanted to see them get better," Heschel recalls. "And the truth is, I *really* liked them. They were great people."

Tonight, seeing Gary and Brianna lying side by side on gurneys, Heschel had wondered what happened to the Narcan she gave them. She later learned paramedics found the couple unconscious in Gary's SUV, the unused bottles in their pockets.

"They'd simultaneously injected large doses of melted-down oxy, topped off with a cap of heroin," Heschel says. "Because they'd overdosed at roughly the same time, neither had time to administer Narcan to the other."

"It's one of the saddest cases I've seen," Heschel adds.

Later, the doctor tends to one of her most difficult duties: calling the families of deceased addicts.

Gary's mother, Frannie Moore, picks up on the first ring.

"Oh, no, no, no," Frannie, 67, yells into the phone. "Not Gary."

"I'm so sorry," Heschel says.

Once Frannie calms down, she tells the doctor she has five children, but that Gary was her only son.

"He's my king," she says. "What am I going to do without him?"

Gary, it turns out, wasn't the first member of the Moore family to die from opiates. Frannie says she'd lost two other relatives to fatal overdoses since the riots: one from pain pills, one from heroin. Both got their drugs from gang-affiliated youngsters, Frannie says, delivery men who'd sold them their fatal doses well under street value.

"It doesn't take a rocket scientist to know where those drugs came from," Frannie says. "A bunch of pharmacies get looted, a bunch of dealers get jacked, and all of a sudden people are overdosing on [drugs] they could never afford before. The way I see it, those riots led to these people's deaths."

Heschel agrees. She tells Frannie the current wave of urban opiate addiction needs more attention from government, the press, and the addiction treatment and medical communities.

"We need to tell people what's happening," Frannie says, "like they're doing in all those white neighborhoods."

"I will," says Heschel. "I'm telling anyone who'll listen."

Back on Oxy Alley, Keisha and Terry are in their usual vacant, readying another shot of oxy.

"Almost good to go," Keisha says, adding a bit more water to their melted-down pills, just like the BGF delivery men had taught her.

"I'm ready, girl," Terry says, her hands beginning to shake, having gone too many hours without a dose. It's raining heavily on Pennsylvania Avenue, lightning illuminating the skies over

West Baltimore. But the weather is of little concern to the
women. All that matters are the next few minutes of uninter-
rupted bliss.

"Yeahhhhhhhh, there it is," Keisha says, slowly pressing
down on the syringe plunger, injecting the oxy little by little,
so as not to take too much at once and overdose. She calls this
method "inching," as opposed to injecting a dose all at once,
which is known as "slamming."

Keisha closes her eyes and smiles, letting the opiates work
their magic. Her son stares at her, transfixed, wondering
what's making his mommy so happy.

To understand what she's feeling, imagine some of life's
greatest pleasures—love, sex, power, wealth, peace of mind—
all rolled into one tiny liquefied pill.

"I've never felt so good in my life," Keisha says. "God bless."

"That nice, huh?" says Terry, sliding the needle from Keisha's vein, both women accustomed by now to sharing "twins,"
or used needles. "I swear, them niggas got the best shit."

Terry draws up the remaining oxy into her syringe, finds
a vein in her left arm, and slams the whole dose home at once.
She wants to get "as high as possible," she says, touching her
stomach, "because this is my last day using, because of my
baby. I swear." It's the same pledge Terry had made—and
quickly broken—five months earlier.

Afterward, as she curls up on the floor beside Keisha, a
fat cockroach ambles past Terry's pregnant belly. And for the
next few hours, the women forget all the ills of life in West
Baltimore—the poverty, the homicides, the mistreatment of
young men like Freddie Gray. They forget about Keisha's
father, Robert, who's serving 10 years in Jessup Correctional
Institution for armed robbery; and Terry's mother, Jaclyn, who

can't afford her HIV medication now that Keisha and Terry have begun raiding her bank account to buy opiates.

They even forget about Moises, who wanders out of the vacant and onto Oxy Alley shortly after 10 p.m. It's another hour before Keisha realizes the six-year-old is gone. Once she does, she rushes out into the night, screaming her son's name.

But he's nowhere in sight.

"Generation Pill"

These [orphaned] children are in Florida, they're in Texas, they're in Missouri, they're in Jersey, they're out west, they're all over. Because the drugs are all over.

—Donna Leonhardt

September 14, 2015, West Baltimore

Derek Curry's posted up outside the Popeye's in Mondawmin, awaiting a Vicodin delivery from BGF, when he spots a bushy-haired little boy crossing the street. He's no older than six, Curry thinks, his purple Transformers shirt ripped in the front, his face covered in a thin layer of filth.

"You lost, little man?" Curry says, wondering where the child's parents are.

Probably getting high somewhere, he figures, just like Curry would be doing if that damned delivery man would get there already. Pill City's drivers are so busy these days, it's taking longer than ever for Curry to get his deliveries.

"You know where you are, son?'

The little boy shrugs, shakes his head, then nods, his eyes wet with tears.

"Dang, that's a lot of answers," says Curry. "What's your name?"

"Moises," the boy says, sniffling. "What's yours?"

"My name's Derek, but everybody calls me D."

"What happened to your eye, D?"

Curry laughs. He'd forgotten how direct children can be, how fearless. He and Cassie had always wanted kids, but she'd died before they got the chance.

"I lost my eye a long time ago, little man, but I'm used to it . . . get by just fine with the one I still got."

Where Curry's eye had once been, there's now a tattered black patch, the same one he's worn for years. He'd lost the orb in a fight with a fellow addict and friend, a man named Otis Washington. Curry and Otis used to be tight, going halves on heroin baggies, pills, and the occasional eight ball of cocaine, until the day Cassie died. Otis had supplied the OxyContin that killed her, and Curry blamed him for her death. The accusation led to a fistfight, during which Otis beat Curry so badly, doctors had no choice but to remove his damaged eye.

"Does it hurt?" says Moises.

"Not even a little," says Curry, who considers the loss of his eye, like his informant work for Detective Grayson, a kind of penance, a way of making up for having let Cassie die on his watch. "One eye makes me special, because everybody else got two."

Looking up, Moises smiles a big, toothy grin, the boy looking so adorable, it makes Curry's heart hurt.

"Moises, where's your mama at right now?"

"She was tired," the child says. "She laid down with Terry."

"Where?"

"That way," he says, pointing north.

"Can you find your way back there?"

Moises shrugs, his eyes going wet again.

Curry makes one last scan of the street, hoping, praying to see a BGF delivery man pulling into the Popeye's parking lot. But there's none in sight. He thinks of what Cassie would have done in this situation: disregard the drug delivery, tend to the little boy, and make sure he gets home safely. She'd have been a great mother, he thinks.

"Come on, little man," Curry says, taking Moises by the hand. "Let's get you back to your mama."

They spend the next two and a half hours searching for Keisha and Terry, but Moises can't remember which street he'd left them on. With Moises exhausted and Curry badly in need of opiates, he decides to take the boy to the Western District station, hopeful that police will help reunite him with Keisha.

"They've got cars and badges, two things we don't," says Curry. "I don't usually deal with police, but in this case, I feel like we got to. Your mama must be panicking."

"I miss her," Moises says, sounding groggy.

At the police station, Curry asks to see Detective Jamal Grayson. But when the desk officer calls down to narcotics, he's told Grayson's on leave, grieving the death of a friend.

"Hold on, I'll get you somebody in CPS [Child Protective Services] instead," the officer says.

Curry hangs around long enough to explain Moises's situation to the CPS worker, but his craving is raging now—his chemical need for opiates too powerful to ignore. He says good-bye to Moises, telling him to "stay brave," then wanders back toward Mondawmin, texting a new drug order to Pill City as he walks. Within the hour, he's holed up in a vacant snorting Vikes, having forgotten all about the boy and his mom.

"Back to the same old," he says.

But for Moises, nothing is the same after that day. He's placed in a state-run group home and, later, with a foster family. The six-year-old is now a member of what some social service workers call "Generation Pill"—children who've seen their lives upended by the opiate epidemic. Some are placed in the care of grandparents and older siblings, authorities say, while others end up with aunts and uncles. Oftentimes, only one relative is financially stable enough to adopt. And when no family members meet that criterion—a frequent occurrence in low-income areas—orphaned children become long-term wards of the state.

Antoine Highland, 15, is another child whose life has been upended by the opiate epidemic's second wave. He's living in Northeast Baltimore with his grandmother Birdie, sleeping in the childhood bedroom of his deceased mother, Janelle Highland. Janelle was found dead of a prescription pill overdose in an East Side vacant in June, a BGF dealer's number saved in her cell phone. Her last words to Antoine were: "I'm going to get better soon."

"I feel like I'm one of the lucky ones," Antoine says, "because they found me a good place to stay after my mom died."

Less fortunate is DeRay Bennett, 14, whose father, Lawrence, died in a New Orleans halfway house in May, the equivalent of 15 high-dose oxys in his system. Lawrence, too, had a BGF dealer's number saved in his phone, along with those for two recovery hotlines. Like many opiate addicts, Lawrence had stolen from his family to buy drugs, thefts that led both of his brothers and all three of his sisters to disown him. When they received calls from the state asking whether they might adopt DeRay, all declined.

"It's not a good feeling, your own blood not wanting you," DeRay recently told a social worker after moving in with yet another foster family.

Like Moises and DeRay, Generation Pill members are often shuffled from one group home or foster family to another—sometimes two or three in the same year. Across the country, at least 266 African American children 17 or younger were orphaned as a result of opiate overdoses in 2015, records show, left to the mercy of overwhelmed, underfunded child welfare agencies.

"There's a whole generation of these kids who lost parents or caretakers to opiates—not only ones prescribed to them by doctors but from these sophisticated drug operations," says Donna Leonhardt, who manages a foster care program in Baltimore and works with the city and state governments to find permanent homes for kids. "These [orphaned] children are in Florida, they're in Texas, they're in Missouri, they're in Jersey, they're out west, they're all over. Because the drugs are all over."

The number of children in America's foster care system as of September 2014 rose 3.5 percent from a year earlier, to 415,129, according to the most recent data compiled by the U.S. Department of Health and Human Services. Those statistics don't track how many kids lost a parent to overdose, but records this reporter reviewed in neighborhoods targeted by Pill City suggest that at least 134 children—most of them 12 or younger—were placed in foster care after a parent died from pills or heroin in 2015.

"These kids' lives won't be the same without that loved one, but we hope to help them gain a semblance of normalcy in the wake of a parent's passing, entry into rehab, or institutionalization," Leonhardt says. "If they're willing to give us a chance, to let us help them, we will work as hard as humanly possible to improve their lives."

Some members of Generation Pill, though, have no say in whether their lives get better—or even whether they survive. These children, authorities say, are the epidemic's "tiniest victims."

"As bad a situation as orphaned kids might be in, they actually have a leg up on kids who are born to opiate-addicted mothers . . . and inherit the addiction itself," said Ronald Percy, an addiction counselor in Staten Island, New York, which has the highest rate of fatal opiate overdoses in New York City. "Not only are they the tiniest victims of [opiate] abuse, they're also the most innocent."

In 2015, Percy treated more than 30 women who gave birth to opiate-addicted children, or "opiate babies," as some clinicians call them. Most say they got their drugs from a Staten Island–based BGF set, Percy says.

"It's bad here for moms," the counselor says. "But it's bad in a lot of other places, too."

The data bears out Percy's claims.

In neighborhoods targeted by Pill City, at least 77* women gave birth to opiate-dependent newborns in 2015, interviews and records show. The problem of dope-sick babies, Percy says, extends back to the opiate epidemic's first wave. Cases of newborn drug dependency—officially known as neonatal abstinence syndrome—increased fivefold between 2000 and 2012, when an estimated 21,732 infants were found to be suffering from the syndrome, according to federal data. Over the past decade, roughly 130,000 babies in the United States

---

* Total is based on author's examination of public and private health records, as well as interviews with opiate addicts, clinicians, and child welfare workers.

have been born with NAS. In America today, an opiate-dependent baby is born every 19 minutes.

"They're born chemically dependent to opiates . . . they're sweating, vomiting, trembling, having diarrhea, as sick as an adult addict might be if they were dope sick, in need of drugs," says Dr. Grace Talbot, a physician and addiction recovery expert at a medical center in St. Louis. "It's very difficult to watch."

In the maternity ward of Chicago's Mercy Hospital, one such baby, Julissa Cromartie, is struggling to breathe tonight, just hours after her premature birth. Her mother, Yvette, a BGF customer and longtime opiate addict, had gone into labor shortly after injecting a boiled-down dose of oxy. The drug numbed Yvette's body so completely, she hadn't sensed anything was amiss until she'd already been in labor for two hours—a period she spent sitting in a convenience store parking lot.

"Somebody help!" the 24-year-old shouted once she realized what was happening.

One of the convenience store clerks called 911 and helped paramedics load Yvette into an ambulance. Twenty-five minutes later, she was in the delivery room at Mercy, her severely underweight daughter inching closer to birth and her opiate high gone.

"She started asking for painkillers the moment they rolled her in," says Julissa's treating physician, Dr. Darryl Lamb. "And it wasn't just because she was in labor. She told us she was an addict, which helped us a great deal with our treatment. But the baby was not her priority at that moment. That's what addiction does to a person's brain . . . it's all-consuming."

Knowing Yvette had opiates in her system, the doctors were "extremely careful" about how much medication they gave her to dull the pain of childbirth, Lamb says. Once Julissa was out of Yvette's womb and in Lamb's arms, the woman didn't ask to hold her baby.

Instead, she reached for her cell phone.

"She wanted to call her [drug] delivery guy," says Lamb. "That was her priority."

Now, standing over Julissa's incubator, Lamb muses over her chances for survival.

"It could go either way for her," Lamb says. If she does survive, he adds, "She'll be addicted for a time, just like her mom. That's what we're seeing more and more of with second-wave addicts."

As hard as Dr. Lamb works to save her, there is no happy ending for Julissa.

Two and a half days after she's born, her heart stops, the toxic payload of opiates her mother consumed, coupled with other serious health problems, too much for the infant to overcome. When Lamb tells Yvette her daughter is gone, she buries her head under her bed sheet and cries herself to sleep.

About the time Julissa's body arrives at a local funeral home, Jimmy Masters is finishing a club soda and lime at his granddaughter's eighth birthday party. Patience is radiant in her white dress, her granddad doting on her while her father, Blackrock, looks on proudly. Not only is his daughter growing into a confident, beautiful girl, Blackrock thinks, but Jimmy is finally back home where he belongs, the whole family beginning to heal after the loss of Stacks and Zeke. Blackrock doesn't know whether his dad is safe here—BGF may still be looking to kill him following their deal with the Carranzas—but he respects Jimmy's decision to be with his only grandchild on her big day.

"Y'all looking sharp out there," Blackrock says, smiling as

his dad and daughter begin to slow dance amid the crowd of partygoers, "It's So Hard to Say Goodbye to Yesterday" playing on the catering hall speakers. Jimmy looks nearly as dapper as he did before Zeke's death, Blackrock thinks, wearing a hand-cut, charcoal gray suit and Italian dress shoes. He seems healthier, too, the rest he's gotten since returning from South America appearing to have made all the difference.

When the DJ changes the track to "Do You Love Me," by The Contours, Blackrock asks to cut in.

"May I have this dance?" he asks Patience.

"Only if Grandpa says it's OK."

"You have my blessing," says Jimmy. "This one's a little fast for my old bones."

The retired kingpin steps outside for some fresh air, while Blackrock twirls his daughter around on the dance floor. Blackrock's thinking about how nice a night they're having—how good it feels to be together again as a family after all they'd endured since April—while his father, breathing in the cool evening air, contemplates whether any of it "means a damn thing at the end of the day."

The song is winding down, and Blackrock is asking his daughter if she's ready to go cut her birthday cake, when shots rings out in the street.

"Stay here, baby," Blackrock says, sprinting out the door. He reaches the sidewalk just in time to see Slim Robinson jumping into Train's Yukon, pistol in hand.

On the ground nearby lies Jimmy Masters, felled by multiple gunshots, his Brooks Brothers button-down shirt soaked in blood.

"I got me *both* brothers now," Slim shouts mockingly from the backseat of Train's SUV, giving Blackrock the middle finger as the BGF gangsters head to their next mission.

"The Interrupters"

If we save even one life, we've changed the world.

—THE REVEREND MARVIN GRIER

Nearing the end of a month when at least 13 opiate-dealing gangsters have been slain or wounded in greater Baltimore, Coach Larry Booker tells his group of volunteers to expect the worst.

"If you see any bullets coming," he says, only half kidding, "you best duck."

Booker is Zeke Masters's old football coach, as talented a motivator of young men as this city has seen. Tonight, he's heading up a different kind of team: a group of recovering opiate addicts, former drug dealers, and grieving parents who have signed up to be "addiction interrupters"—activists who have answered the coach's call to take "prayer-inspired action" to combat the opiate epidemic ravaging Baltimore. Their goal this evening: find those contributing to the current wave of addiction and murder, then "interrupt" the cycle.

Booker, whose daughter Brittany died of a painkiller overdose a decade ago, making him part of what he calls "Baltimore's biggest, saddest club," hands each interrupter a reflective orange vest, the words "Life Saver" emblazoned on the front. Tonight is the group's first "prayer patrol," the coach says. If it's successful, they plan to conduct at least two a week.

"We're going to put these vests on so that people know we're here to help them—not to mess with their high, or take them to jail," Booker says of the assorted gangsters, addicts, slingers, and prostitutes who do business along Oxy Alley. His team of activists is modeling its efforts on those of "violence interrupters," reformed gang members who patrol dangerous stretches of Chicago, New York, and numerous other cities in an effort to prevent bloodshed. Those interrupters treat violence as a communicable disease to be prevented, like AIDS or Ebola. And Booker thinks the same strategy can help combat opiate addiction.

"We want to talk to people, to pray with people, and tell them they're not alone out here, because they truly are suffering from a disease, an ailment of the brain," explains Booker, 62, who's wearing an Orioles cap, khaki pants, and neon green Nikes, "so that the gangsters see how slow I'm moving . . . that I'm just an old coach, not a gangster, and don't mistake me for a threat."

He adds: "If anybody says they don't want us here, if anybody threatens us or shows us a weapon, we simply move on to the next block. But if there's a chance at saving lives, of making a difference, we stay put. We make a connection. We show them there are people out here who care."

With a hot wind whipping up garbage along Pennsylvania Avenue, the interrupters begin their patrol, Booker leading the way. They pass a barefoot child in a syringe-strewn yard, exchange waves with a pregnant teenager gazing longingly out her bedroom window, and nod toward the addicts and dealers milling around a popular drug corner.

"So much despair," says Patrice Dunhill, an interrupter whose daughter, Robyn, died of a Vicodin overdose in May 2015, a few blocks south of Oxy Alley. "That's why we're out here tonight, to try and make things just a little less painful for folks. Lord knows, this street could use the help."

When Dunhill was young, Pennsylvania Avenue had been a ritzy thoroughfare, she says, renowned for its world-class clubs featuring entertainers like Billie Holliday, Ella Fitzgerald, and Thelonious Monk. She had watched a number of acts perform here, she says, including local jazz guitarist–turned-addict Derek Curry, whom Dunhill still sees roaming these streets on occasion, wearing his dusty eye patch.

"Believe it or not," says Dunhill, "Pennsylvania was once the place to see and be seen. Now? It's a place to go when you run out of chances."

The avenue lost much of its luster in April 1968, when Dr. Martin Luther's King's assassination triggered riots across the city, leaving six people dead and nearly 700 injured. More than 1,000 businesses were robbed or damaged during the unrest, but nowhere was the devastation more profound than along Pennsylvania. Rioters there scorched businesses, looted buildings, and clashed violently with cops. And while violence rocked other cities after King's death, most of their major thoroughfares recovered.

Pennsylvania never did.

Today, the street embodies a legacy of inequality plaguing America's poorest inner-city neighborhoods: places where the block people are born on largely determines how far they'll go in life: from what kind of education or job they'll get to whether they'll die from a stray bullet. Neighborhoods like these aren't mere accidents; they're the result of decades of discriminatory housing policies and racial covenants, a seemingly endless War on Drugs, and the perpetual underfunding of key institutions— from schools and public hospitals to health departments and addiction treatment programs.

"Ain't nothing changed around here but the faces and the number of houses abandoned," says another interrupter, the Reverend Marvin Grier, a lifelong friend of Coach Booker's. "Seems like there's more of both every year."

Grier, 69, has been walking these blighted blocks since the 1960s—first as a slinger, now as a clergyman. This is the street where he'd sold his first bag of dope, the neighborhood where he'd plied his trade before flying to San Diego for what was supposed to be a major heroin deal.

But things hadn't gone as planned.

Grier's West Coast customers gave him half of what they owed up front—just over $1 million. When it came time to hand over the rest of the cash, the buyers balked. An ensuing shoot-out between the crews left two people dead and landed Grier in San Quentin. Luckily for him, the cops never recovered that first million—money the reverend is rumored to still be living on today.

Now, clutching a Bible, Grier makes his way into one of the many vacants lining Pennsylvania, places where addicts keep company with bats, rats, and roaches, getting high in rooms blanketed in graffiti and grime. The reverend—slowed by arthritis and cataracts, but still in possession of those sparking green eyes and resonant voice—spots a man huddled in the corner of the home, head nodding, eyes flickering.

"Don't mean to intrude on you, sir," Grier says, the addict

stirring at the sound of his voice, "but we're wondering if you'd be so kind as to let us pray with you."

"Who's that?" the man says, squinting into the glare of Grier's reflective vest. "Po-lice?"

"No, far from it," says Grier. "Just friends here to help."

The activists introduce themselves, each one shaking the addict's hand while he gets his bearings. He says his name is Otis Washington and that he lives "right here on the alley," sleeping in a "different vacant most every night." A former sanitation worker, Otis says he'd blown his life savings and social security checks on heroin, pain pills, coke, and any other drugs he could procure. But none of it's "been much fun" since the falling out he'd had with his friend Derek Curry following Cassie Curry's overdose death. The men used to "look out for each other," Otis says, "but these days, I'm a solo show.

"This is my job now," Otis adds, tapping the festering sores on his arm. "This is who I am."

"Otis, I know that isn't true," says Booker, helping the addict to his feet, then leading him out of the stifling vacant. "Those drugs are just drugs, not who you are."

Otis looks around at the activists gathered on the street. In the three decades he's been an addict, these are the first people who have treated him like "a real human being," he says.

"We want to help you as best we can, Otis," says Grier. "But first, we'd like to pray with you, let the Lord help you out a little. Will you join us?"

Otis weighs the proposal, trying to recall the last time he stepped foot in a church.

"Why not?" he says. "A little praying never hurt no one, far as I know."

The activists form a circle and join hands, the air around

them thick with marijuana smoke wafting from open windows and doorways along the alley.

"Dear God," Grier begins, his voice deep and melodic, honed from years of street-corner sermons, "we ask that you deliver our brother Otis from the grip of addiction and dependence, that you save him from the disease that has infected our communities and bring him comfort in his time of need."

The reverend nods at Booker, signaling him to pick up the prayer.

"We ask you, Jesus, that you visit your grace and healing touch upon our brother Otis," Booker says, the other activists shouting "yes" and "amen," urging the coach to "speak that truth."

"He has so much to give to our wonderful city," the coach continues. "Won't you please walk with him, and all those suffering in Baltimore tonight?"

Booker's no preacher, but he remains a highly effective leader and organizer—skills he had developed during nearly four decades of coaching. He had held many positions over the years: linebackers' coach for a Canadian Football League team; assistant coaching stints at several Division II colleges; and head coaching gigs at several high schools in Maryland and Virginia, where he had helped hundreds of young men steer clear of the drug game. Tonight, Booker knows, his team will gauge its success by a different metric: the number of lives saved.

But not everyone's on board with their mission.

That truth is thrown into stark relief when a crowd of angry-looking BGF members, stumbling addicts, and a miniskirt-clad prostitute moves toward the interrupters' prayer circle, muttering complaints.

"Niggas need to keep walking," one dealer says.

"We don't need these fools out here, messing with our money," adds the prostitute.

Grier, undeterred, continues the prayer.

"We ask you, Jesus, to release Otis from the temptations and dangers that have made this neighborhood such a difficult place for so many, for so long," the street preacher says, his voice growing louder with each word. "Please, Lord, walk with Otis, help Otis heal, guide him onto a better path. And please, God, walk with us, too. Protect my brothers and sisters as we try and bring your will into the heart of this broken community tonight, amen."

"Amen!" the interrupters shout, each of them embracing Otis in turn, thanking him for his time.

Afterward, Grier and Booker hand Otis a bag filled with peanut butter and jelly sandwiches, along with a folder fat with government forms: applications for social services, addiction treatment programs, and housing subsidies. Last, they give him a disposable cell phone programed with both their numbers. The coach and pastor will be Otis's "recovery guides," they explain, helping him fill out paperwork, procure a government ID, and enter rehab—but only if he's willing.

"I am willing, Lord knows," he says, cognizant of the ever-growing crowd of gangsters and addicts gathered around them. "This ain't no place for me to be anymore."

"Good, then we'll be back here tomorrow to help you fill these out, and every day after that, as long as it takes to get you set up," Grier says. "And you call either of these numbers whenever you need something, or if you just feel like talking. That work for you?"

Otis nods, placing a hand on his heart.

"Thank you a thousand times for this," he says, wishing

he'd found the group years earlier, before he'd given those pills to Cassie Curry.

"No need to thank us," says Booker. "Just stay positive, my man. You ain't alone."

Otis heads back into his preferred vacant, wanting to steer clear of the gangsters assembling outside, while the interrupters walk deeper into Oxy Alley, stopping every few minutes to pray with addicts and residents, the homeless and mentally ill, and anyone else open to their presence there.

"Fuck y'all think you doing?" The question is shouted from a BGF member, one of 15 or so gangsters now gathered in the street.

"We just praying with folks, trying to help out whoever needs it," says Booker, sensing trouble for the first time tonight.

"That don't concern me none," the same gangster says.

If the interrupters take off now, Booker thinks, they'll lose the respect of everyone in these streets, making their work there that much harder. So, rather than retreat, the coach walks right up to the gangster who had yelled at him—the biggest, meanest-looking hustler in the group—and offers a hand in greeting.

As he does, Booker's taken aback by the gangster's face.

"Desmond?"

"Damn, it's been a minute," the gangster says, smiling as he recognizes his high school football coach. "I don't miss them two-a-days, but glad to see you holding up aight."

Booker can hardly believe it: Desmond Vickers, formerly his star fullback, is now running with Baltimore's BGF set, the most ruthless drug gang in the city. "Damage," as his teammates dubbed him, was once among Booker's best players: an agile, intelligent athlete whose blocking skills and speed in the open field were so impressive, he had been scouted by several Division I schools.

But instead of attending college, he had immersed himself in the drug game—a decision he claims he's never regretted, given the amount of money he's earned. And yet, seeing the disappointment in his ex-coach's eyes, Damage can't help but wonder what might have been.

"It's good to see you, young man," Booker says. "You're looking strong as ever."

The gangsters and activists all shake hands, the tension that existed moments earlier dissipated. Damage asks the group whether they understand the risk they are taking by marching through Oxy Alley at this hour, given the "number of fiends and stickup boys we got running around this time of night."

"We do understand, absolutely," Grier says. "We're just trying to do the work of the Lord in these streets, whatever the dangers."

Damage says that's fine by him, so long as they stay out of the gang's way.

"Y'all ain't got nothing to worry about with us," says Booker. "Way we see it, we all in this together, as a community."

Damage agrees. But in doing so, he's acting contrary to Lyric's orders. For as soon as the set leader got wind of Grier's presence in Oxy Alley that night, he had phoned his field marshal with instructions to "put a bullet in that nigga . . . [to] send a message" to the activists. Instead, Damage had watched and waited, observing the interrupters in action. Now that he knows Coach Booker's in charge, there's no way he's going to harm the reverend.

But Slim and Train have other ideas.

The men come tearing down the block in Train's Yukon, pulling up alongside their fellow gangsters.

"What these Al Sharpton mothafuckers doing on our block?" Slim shouts, stepping bare-chested out of the SUV, his shirt having been splashed with Jimmy Masters's blood.

Booker examines the tattoos on the gangster's chest, several rows of tiny skulls, and wonders what they signify.

Grier, though, knows exactly what they mean.

"That's a whole lot of souls you going to have to answer for," he says of the tattoos, a long-standing BGF tradition. Each of the 12 or so skulls represents a life Slim had taken—in Baltimore, Iraq, and elsewhere.

"Oh, I heard you was here, Reverend," Slim says, making the last word sound like an insult. "But you ain't supposed to be. This a [BGF] corner."

Slim is well aware of Grier's history, both as a heroin dealer and a Black Power activist. He's heard about the drug money Grier supposedly has stashed away, along with his frequent sermons condemning BGF.

"I go wherever the spirit moves me," says Grier. "Not like you all, preying on poor people, going wherever there's money to be made."

"Shit, I don't see you worrying about that money *you* made slinging back in the day . . . that cash you still living on," Slim says. "Way I see it, you a fucking hypocrite."

Booker steps between the men, as if to intervene, but Grier waves him off.

"Maybe you're right," the reverend says, "but when I was running [with BGF], it was to make things better for our people—not worse. But you . . . you don't cause nothing but pain. You lower than low, son."

"Keep talking, mothafucker," Slim says. He moves quickly

toward Train's Yukon, where a pair of pistols are stashed in the glove box. "I'mma show you how we do."

Just then, a trio of police cars pulls up, responding to reports of a fight in the area.

"Aw, shit," Slim says, his hand already clutching one of the pistol's grips.

The cops arrest him and Train for gun possession, Slim shouting threats as he's pushed into the backseat of a squad car.

"I'mma see you," he yells at Grier, but the reverend, already chatting up the next addict in need, doesn't pay him any mind.

An hour later, Booker walks through his front door, his back aching worse than it ever did in his coaching days.

"Lord, what a night," he says, touching a hand to the framed photographs resting on his dresser. One picture is of his wife, Marilyn, who'd died of breast cancer seven years earlier. The other is of his 18-year-old daughter, Brittany, who'd suffered a fatal overdose just hours after graduating high school. She'd consumed a lethal mix of alcohol, Percocet, and OxyContin while at a house party with friends, dying in her prettiest party dress, a small gold crucifix dangling from her neck.

That was a decade ago, but the memory of Brittany's death is never far from Booker's mind.

"Tomorrow's her birthday, you know," the coach says, gazing at his daughter's picture. "I'm just trying to honor her memory best as I can. That's why I started this interrupter [group]."

For a long time, Booker says, he wasn't sure how to "harness all this pain, this tremendous hole I felt had been carved out in the middle of my heart." The grief of losing his only child left him so distraught, Booker says, he couldn't continue coaching. That same "ocean of hurt" consumed his wife, who was diagnosed with cancer a few years after Brittany's death.

"I felt completely lost without them," says Booker, who credits the Reverend Grier's support with helping him cope with suicidal thoughts during that "very scary, very dark period.

"Marvin helped me get through my worst days. He said, 'God needs your help with something, that's why he's keeping you around.' But I couldn't imagine what God could possibly want with me. I just wanted to be with my daughter and wife, whatever I had to do to get there."

It stayed like that for years, Booker spending most of his time alone watching TV or else flipping through old photo albums. His friends, including the reverend, weren't sure he'd ever overcome his grief.

Then, after the riots, something changed.

Booker saw a number of his neighbors and ex-players dying from opiate overdoses, with others, like Zeke, getting killed in gangland disputes. He says he watched with rising alarm as cops "withdrew" from crime-plagued neighborhoods in response to the riots, giving Pill City and other criminal operations more room to operate.

"People started overdosing like I've never seen, getting shot like I've never seen . . . people dying in their own homes, outside their homes, in their bedrooms, bathrooms, in the park, in the streets," Booker says. "It was all these drugs and violence that the riots unloosed, like a storm."

Alarmed by the chaos engulfing his city, Booker went to hear one of Grier's Sunday sermons, hoping for a little guidance. The reverend, he says, didn't disappoint.

"Marvin was talking about all the people we were losing to drugs, how we had a duty to do something about it," says the coach. "I very quickly realized God might have kept me around so that I could try and save some of these people, maybe as a way to make penance for what happened to Brittany."

He continues: "I'd spent a long time blaming myself for losing my daughter, playing the old 'what if?' game. What if I'd talked to her more about drugs, about not touching any of that poison? Which I *did* do, but maybe not enough. What if I'd told her to just come home, instead of letting her hang with her friends that night? That would have saved her, too.

"But I didn't do those things, and I've accepted that . . . I've got to live with that. Organizing this [interrupter] group to try and save folks . . . that was something I could do to honor her, to turn all this grief I've felt into something positive. Marvin once said to me, 'If we save even one life, we've changed the world.' And that's stayed with me."

For the past three months, Booker has been recruiting volunteers from across the city, assembling what he calls a "God-fearing team" of recovering addicts, ex-dealers, and grieving parents who, like him, want to "turn grief into action."

With his daughter's birthday looming, he had been scrambling to organize the group's maiden march, "since that was the best present I could think of for my baby."

"And thank God, we just barely made it," Booker says, touching his daughter's photograph one last time before going to bed.

The morning after Slim and Train's arrests on weapons charges, Lyric posts bail for both men, cash not an issue now that BGF's "getting money like Trump," the set leader says.

After driving the freed gangsters back to Train's Yukon, Lyric immediately phones Brick.

"We need to talk about your cousin, yo," Lyric says, still

stewing over Damage's refusal to shoot Grier. "That nigga tripping."

Brick, who typically deals with his cousin on issues pertaining to BGF, is surprised to hear from the set leader. Plus, he's in no mood to be taking calls.

"Why you getting at me with this?" Brick says, sounding exhausted. "You should talk to my cuz yourself, see what's up."

The Pill City cofounder is still in bed at 4 p.m. on a Wednesday, severely depressed after a weekslong manic upswing. The last thing he wants right now is to get mixed up in an intragang dispute. But Lyric doesn't relent.

"I tried talking to him but . . . we long past that point," says Lyric. "I'm actually hoping *you* could get with him, talk some sense into his stubborn ass. Either that, or we going to have to find some other solution."

The implication, Brick thinks, is clear: Either Damage gets in line voluntarily, or he's going to be harmed by his own gang.

"Yo, you know that man's my blood, right?" Brick says.

"I know, and I don't mean no disrespect," says Lyric. "I'm asking for your help because I think you a smart mothafucker. And I respect what you did over at Zey's."

The killings of Zey and Victoria Walker were a boon to Brick's reputation, he knows, as good for him as they were bad for Wax, who'd been visibly shaken by the murders. Damage did exactly what BGF's franchise leaders asked of him that night: He ensured that Brick and Wax "got their hands dirty." Still, Lyric continues to distrust his field marshal, believing he'll never be as loyal to him as he was to Red. Damage's refusal to put a bullet in Grier last night was just the latest example.

"All I can say is, that shit's between y'all," Brick says.

It seems for a moment like Lyric's going to drop the issue.

"I understand, yo," the set leader says. Then he tries a different tack.

"I know you and your cuz tight and all, but honestly, I feel like I need to tell you something . . . about some shit he been talking."

"Nigga, you tripping."

"Nah, but I wish I was."

"What did my cousin say, then?"

"He said you was . . . shit, I don't even know how to say this . . . he said you got straight-up raped by that nigga Arthur Kane back in the day."

The statement shocks Brick, his chest tightening as memories of Arthur's abuse come rushing back. The shame he feels is so immense, he thinks of suicide; not *whether* he can go through with it, but how quickly. It's the "bad" side of his bipolar talking, he knows, but the thought is of little comfort.

"I don't mean to drag up shit from the past," Lyric says. "But I thought you should know."

Lyric's motives are far from pure. He's hoping to drive a wedge between Brick and Damage, thinking the field marshal's influence within Pill City will be diminished if he loses his younger cousin's trust. Lyric also recognizes Brick's potential to become a skilled enforcer in his own right, having already dispatched the Walkers. Lyric could use another loyal assassin, especially if he's successful in further marginalizing Damage.

"This foul, yo," Brick says.

"Don't even sweat this, my nigga," Lyric says, asking if he can swing by Brick's apartment, maybe bring him something to eat. "Right now, you need to be around somebody you can trust."

Feeling lower than he's ever felt, Brick mumbles his address. A half hour later, Lyric arrives at his door, clutching two bags of burgers and fries.

"Keep your head up, bruh," Lyric says, hugging Brick as though they were old friends. "Everything going to work out . . . trust me."

"Going Dark"

Unfortunately, the law hasn't kept pace with technol-
ogy, and this disconnect has created a significant pub-
lic safety problem.

—FBI DIRECTOR JAMES COMEY

"These guys, they're a bunch of fucking nobodies."

Detective Grayson is sitting at his desk in the Western District station, riffling through a folder thick with mug shots of looting suspects. He's spent three days flashing these images around Baltimore, showing them to pharmacists, police informants, opiate addicts, and anyone else with an eye on the streets. So far, his efforts have led to six arrests, mostly of low-level BGF slingers on charges unrelated to the pharmacy lootings. But his real targets—Brick and Wax—remain free, their true identities a mystery.

"We've got nothing on the actual syndicate [leaders], the guys who run the tech side . . . no physical description, no age range, no last known address, nothing to really work with beyond the BGF links," the detective says on this his fifth day back at work since returning from leave. "It's frustrating to know as little as we do about them," he says of Pill City, "when people are out there dying."

Of all those deaths, Grayson says, it's Patti's that hurts most.

He thinks about her "every hour of every day," he says, imagining the various ways he might have saved her life: a few kind words before hanging up the phone, a promise to see her again once she finished addiction treatment, even a short visit to her home that night to wish her good luck.

"Any of those things could have stopped it," Grayson says of Patti's oxycodone overdose. "But I was worried about compromising the case. I thought the investigation was more important than a human being."

At Patti's funeral, her father, Fred Sinclair, had urged Grayson not to blame himself.

"But I let her down, I really did," Grayson replied.

"That's a bunch of nonsense," the pharmacist said. "She admired you. Nothing you said or did was going to do anything to that woman but make her happy."

Fred explained that Patti was a depressive with a long history of drug and alcohol abuse. Her ex-husband, the private investigator, had physically and emotionally abused her, in addition to turning her on to pills. And Patti "never got over" her mother's death in 2014, Fred said.

"It had nothing to do with you, Jamal," he insisted. "Patti had her own demons she was dealing with."

Now, Grayson's dealing with his.

He's been drinking copious amounts of Budweiser and Jameson of late—alcohol "the only thing that lets me sleep," Grayson says. At work, his colleagues have noticed a change in him; the way he's "doubling down" on his obsessive tendencies, Malinowski says. Since returning from leave, Grayson has been working 16-hour days, driving himself so hard, Malinowski has suggested he take *another* leave of absence, that he "go lay on the beach somewhere and forget about everything." But when Grayson tried to plan a visit with his sons in California earlier in the year, his ex-wife told him they were gone for the summer, touring the West Coast with their stepdad.

So instead of traveling, Grayson keeps at his work, believing that the only way to redeem himself, to assuage his guilt, is to take down the dealers who'd sold Patti her fatal dose.

"I made a conscious decision that night I spoke with [Patti] . . . to not jeopardize the case," Grayson says. "If it was that important to me then, I've got to see it through now."

Six days later, Grayson and Malinowski catch a break.

It comes as they're sitting in an interrogation room in the Western District station, grilling one of BGF's most ruthless enforcers, Dome Simmons.

"You got to work with us here, Lionel, give us some kind of reason to help you," Malinowski says, reminding Dome he'd already served two prison stints for drug dealing. "Ain't you done enough time?"

"Man, I already told you, I ain't shot *nobody*."

"Yeah, he just fell into your nine [millimeter]," Grayson says.

Dome's been in custody nearly two hours, hauled in for questioning in the shooting of Shomari "Kapo" Jones, 19, an independent dealer who, like so many of his slinger brethren, took a bullet for the crime of hustling in Pill City territory. Kapo remains hospitalized, with a single gunshot wound to his torso, and is likely to survive. But his condition is less important to Grayson than the results of a pending ballistics test, one the detective hopes will definitely link Dome to Kapo's shooting and give the enforcer more incentive to cooperate with detectives against Pill City's leaders.

"We know you hit Kapo," says Malinowski. "But you give us something on [Pill City], that charge maybe gets [downgraded] to assault. And you stay out of Jessup."

Dome, after a long silence, says he *does* have some information to share after all.

Both detectives lean forward in their chairs, eager to hear what the ex-con will reveal. But instead of tipping them off to Brick and Wax's true identities or giving them the name of Jimmy and Zeke's killer, Dome leans back in his chair and says: "Fuck you, Detectives."

Grayson wants nothing more than to lay the gangster out, wipe that stupid smile off his face with a haymaker to his jaw. But the detective's always been a by-the-book cop; he's never struck a suspect, he says, and he's not about to start now.

Instead of clocking Dome, he tells him he admires his unwillingness to snitch.

"Everybody's got some kind of code, right?" Grayson says.

A little later, outside the interrogation room, the detective feels his iPhone vibrating. He digs it out of his pocket, recognizing the crime lab's number on the caller ID.

"Please tell me we got a match," Grayson says.

But the analyst on the other end has mixed news: The pistol recovered from Dome's car during a traffic stop this morning *might* be the one used to shoot Kapo, or it might not be. The initial test, he says, is inconclusive.

After Grayson shares the news with Malinowski, the sergeant marches right back into the interrogation room and tells Dome the guns *do* match, conclusively.

Misleading suspects during an interrogation is legal, Malinowski knows, and often effective.

"Damn," Dome says, his swagger fading, knowing a deal with the cops might be the only way to avoid another bid in Jessup.

He weighs his options for another hour, then utters a line that's music to the detectives' ears: "You help me, I'll help you, aight?"

Dome's cooperation could break the drug looting case "wide open," Grayson says later that day. The gangster has promised to give investigators everything they want on Pill City's leaders—names, locations, and a sworn statement detailing their operations. In return, he wants to spend no more than six months behind bars.

Grayson says such a deal would be unnecessary—that the police and DEA would undoubtedly be farther along in their investigation by now—if it weren't for smartphone encryption. Time and again, he says, investigators have secured warrants to search iPhones belonging to BGF dealers and other Pill City associates—including Dome—only to find the devices protected by the same technology now being used by ISIS terrorists.

"In the past, we'd have asked the [cell phone] carriers to help on a case like this," Grayson says. But now that new Apple and Android devices come standard with encryption features, police, federal authorities, and the technology companies themselves typically cannot access a phone's data, officials say, even when a search warrant is issued.

"It used to be a drug dealer's phone contained all the information we needed to nail a guy," says Malinowski. "Incriminating messages, voicemails, phone numbers of higher-level traffickers, associates, customers . . . everything was in that phone, because a drug dealer's world revolves around his phone. Now, in many cases, we have no way of accessing that world. Their phones are warrant-proof."

Kirstin Marques, the DEA agent, says the standardization of encryption features on smartphones is "just about the worst thing that's ever happened to drug investigators, and that's not hyperbole.

"It's created a situation where we're playing the game with one hand tied behind our backs," Marques adds. "The dealers know the new iPhones are encrypted, and they're using them to hide their dirt.

"Even more disconcerting," she adds, "is that they're using encryption far more frequently, and with far greater consequences, than terrorists do."

At the highest levels of government, fierce debates have played out over whether tech giants like Apple and Google should build "back doors" into their networks, so that law enforcement can access the smartphones of suspected criminals. Tech companies have resisted such a move, arguing it would leave customer data vulnerable to malicious hackers, identity thieves, and foreign governments. In the most striking example of corporate pushback, Apple refused to help the FBI open a locked iPhone used by one of the terrorists who killed 14 people in San Bernardino, California, in December 2015. The FBI eventually found a way to crack the phone without Apple's help, paying professional hackers to exploit a previously overlooked security flaw.

"Unfortunately, the law hasn't kept pace with technology, and this disconnect has created a significant public safety problem," James Comey, the FBI director, has said. "We call it 'going dark,' and what it means is this: Those charged with protecting our people aren't always able to access the evidence we need to prosecute crime . . . we have the legal authority to intercept and access communications and information pursuant to court order, but we often lack the technical ability to do so."

Now that Dome's agreed to cooperate, the issue of encryption might end up being moot, Marques tells Grayson.

"Sometimes, the old-fashioned way still works," she says.

"Or so we hope," says Grayson.

The next morning, Dome is arraigned on a weapons possession charge, then released on bail posted by his mother. Although they can't legally hold him any longer, Dome agrees to meet with Malinowski, Marques, and Grayson at the Western District station, but first, he says, he wants to go home and take a nap.

"Is this guy playing us?" Malinowski asks, wondering if the nap story is a ruse.

"I hope not," says Grayson. "But he's all we got, and he knows it."

Dome tells the investigators he's going to "pass out" for "two, maybe three hours," then head straight to the Western with his attorney. But when Grayson calls Dome to remind him his three hours are up, there's no answer. He phones again every 20 minutes, always with the same result.

"We better go over there," Malinowski says. "Lord knows what this guy's up to."

When he and Grayson arrive at Dome's apartment, the place is in disarray, furniture strewn about the place, the door lock busted.

"Somebody got to him," Grayson says.

That theory is confirmed nine days later when Dome's body, badly decayed, is found in suburban Virginia. Whoever shot the BGF enforcer had disposed of his corpse in shallow water, just beyond the boundaries of a state park. The hiker who found him told detectives he had simply "followed the smell" along the water's edge, until he saw a gold chain glistening beneath the surface, attached to a bloated body.

When Grayson learns of Dome's fate, he puts his head in his hands, thinking of Patti.

"How many people," he asks Malinowski, "have to die for our mistakes?"

"A Deadly Migration"

Once the heroin takes over, you're finished. My baby girl was finished.

—RONNIE VOORHEES

October 15, 2015, South Florida

The heroin arrives in Riviera Beach shortly after 2 a.m., and, like most of Pill City's illicit cargo outside Baltimore, it's immediately unloaded into a rented storage space. Royal Monroe and Deuce Fenton have driven the drugs here from Maryland without incident, "probably because I'm driving a rented Prius and dressed preppy, looking like Obama and shit," Royal says. The syndicate's drivers usually wear a dress shirt and tie on out-of-state trafficking trips, a strategy Train says he's implemented to help fool highway cops.

"How was the drive?" asks Deron "Niko" Walters, leader of the Riviera Beach BGF set, also known as the Get Money Everyday Clique. "Y'all stop to see any of the sights?"

Royal and Deuce look at each other quizzically, unsure whether the set leader is serious.

"You know, like tourist-type shit?" Niko says.

"Yo, we just trying to deliver this shit and get the fuck out of here," says Royal, who, like Deuce, is exhausted from their 15-hour drive. They'd taken turns behind the wheel, never going faster than the posted speed limit, per Train's orders.

"'Nuff said," says Niko, helping the Baltimoreans carry the last of their heroin bricks into the storage space. "Y'all all about that business, all professional like. I respect that shit."

Niko, even by South Florida standards, is a "funny-looking dude," Royal thinks. He's wearing a flamingo-pink football jersey emblazoned with the number 516—Riviera Beach's area code—along with yellow high-tops and a multicolor do-rag. The gear is far from inconspicuous, hardly the ideal outfit for a nighttime re-up, the Baltimore gangsters think. But the Get Money Everyday Clique has its own way of doing things, as do each of BGF's sets around the country. Niko's been a Pill City franchisee since May, the partnership earning him and his gang more than $300,000 in profits. Now the group is making the transition from prescription opiate sales to heroin, having recently exhausted its inventory of stolen painkillers.

"Nigga looked like the ghetto Liberace," Royal says once they're back on the highway,

"To each his own, though," says Deuce. "Long as that money right, nigga can dress like Mickey Mouse if he feels like it."

The Baltimore gangsters gone, Niko examines the newly arrived heroin, rubbing his hands together like a kid on Christmas morning.

"So much money to be made here, it's crazy," he says.

The following afternoon, he and his lieutenants cut the heroin with baking soda, then funnel the adulterated product into hundreds of twist-top baggies. Afterward, the drugs are distributed to three different corner crews, each consisting of four or five clique members. Two of those crews use Pill City's text-to-order software to coordinate drug deliveries, Niko says. The third makes open-air sales on street corners in Riviera Beach's poorest areas.

"That way, we get the door-to-door business *and* the walk-up and drive-through crowds," Niko says. "In this market, you need to do both [deliveries and corner sales] to be successful."

The strategy is a marked departure from that of their BGF counterparts in Baltimore, who, shortly after the April riots, transitioned to a delivery-only model in an effort to avoid police surveillance.* Corner sweeps—in which cops roll up on a drug corner and arrest every dealer and customer in sight—are conducted far more frequently in Baltimore than they are in Riviera Beach, Niko says. As a result, his gang has more flexibility than many other Pill City franchises when it comes to sales tactics.

"Part of what makes the [franchise] model so smart," Niko says, "is that everybody can do business the way they want, cater to their own kinds of customers."

One of the first locals to buy heroin from Niko's set is Leon Marion, a 19-year-old community college student and aspiring paramedic and firefighter. Leon has just completed his final exams for the semester and is looking to relax this weekend, he says, maybe take some oxycodone with his girlfriend, Tasha, in advance of their upcoming vacation in Puerto Rico.

But when Leon drives up to his usual drug corner, the Get Money Everyday Clique dealer on duty, Jayvon Strong, tells him they're out of pills.

---

* Baltimore has one of the largest closed-circuit camera systems in the country. In January 2016, the city's surveillance capabilities were expanded when police partnered with a private company that flew surveillance missions over Baltimore, recording hundreds of hours of footage.

"All we got is raw."

"Raw?"

"Yeah, heroin."

"Oh, shit. How much that cost?"

"Ten a bag, or three for 20."

Leon weighs whether to make a buy, knowing the high from heroin is supposed to be almost identical to that from oxy. For the better part of a year, he's been scoring pills on this corner once or twice a week. But he'd never injected a drug before.

"You got to shoot it?" Leon asks.

"Nah, you can snort it if you want," says Jayvon. "Like coke."

"All right, I'll do three," Leon says, figuring he better get that extra bag, in case Tasha wants to try some. He hands two $10 bills to Jayvon, who directs him to a red-roofed house on the next block. There, another dealer retrieves three twist-top bags from beneath a plastic garbage bin and hands them to Leon.

"Thanks," the college student says.

Excited by the prospect of trying dope for the first time, he drives straight home, locks his bedroom door behind him, and snorts a thick line of powder off his computer desk. In a few minutes, he's feeling "mellow and warm, high as hell," he says, forgetting all about the fire department entrance exam scheduled a little over two months from that day.

Leon turns on his TV, flipping through channels until he lands on a *Sopranos* rerun. Then he snorts another line, nodding off in bed. A little later, he hears his dad and stepmom come home from dinner, bickering as usual. The house is too small for the three of them, Leon thinks. As soon as he gets back from Puerto Rico with Tasha, he plans to move into her place, maybe even get engaged.

"Leon, you eat yet?" his stepmom shouts from the living room. "We've got leftovers if you're hungry."

"I'm good," he bellows through the closed bedroom door, trying hard not to slur his words.

It's after sundown when Leon's phone rings, stirring him from his heroin stupor. It's Tasha, calling to ask where he's been.

"I've been trying you for like four hours," she says, sounding sexy as usual, Leon thinks. He checks the time on his iPhone and sees it's 8:37. He was supposed to at her place at 6:30 for dinner.

"I lost track of time," Leon says. "I'll come over there right now . . . make it up to you."

Tasha can tell from Leon's voice that he's high.

"You taking pills without me?" she says.

"Nah, baby, I got something better," Leon says. "Let me come through and show you."

He's out the door five minutes later, but not before snorting another line for the road.

In the street, Leon stumbles over to his car, struggling to fit the key in the driver's side door lock. On his way to Tasha's, he realizes he's got only one bag of heroin left.

"Shit won't do," he says, making a U-turn and driving back to Jayvon's corner.

"My man, I knew you'd like it," Jayvon says when Leon rolls up. "Shit is right, huh?"

"Hell yeah," Leon says, forking over two more $10 bills. "Let me get another three bags."

Heroin in hand, he races toward Tasha's, hoping he can talk her into trying on the new bikini she had purchased for the trip.

But he's quickly disabused of that notion.

"You look *all* messed up," she says soon as she opens the door.

Leon's swaying back and forth on her front porch, eyes bloodshot, a trio of tiny white flakes stuck to his nostrils. "What are you on?"

He pulls a bag from his pocket and dangles it in front of Tasha's face.

"H? Oh, hell no," she says. "I'm not touching that mess."

"You're going to love it, I promise."

Tasha reminds him that her father had been a heroin addict before he ran out on her mom. She had vowed never to let the stuff inside her own home after seeing what it did to her dad.

"Pills one thing, Leon. H something else."

"Fine, just let me come in then," he says, grabbing at her backside.

Tasha knocks his hand away.

"Not while you're high," she says.

"Damn, what I come over here for then?" Leon slurs.

"I don't know, but you need to get rid of that," Tasha says, pointing at the baggie. "I'm serious. I won't be around it."

Leon waves a hand at her and stumbles back to his car, eager to get home and snort another line.

"You need to relax, girl," he shouts as he peels away from Tasha's place. "Life's too short not to try new things."

Riffling through his stepmom's purse the following night, Leon tells himself it's no big deal; he'll slip the cash back into her wallet soon as his next financial aid check arrives. He grabs a $20 bill, drives to the BGF corner, and buys himself three more bags of raw.

"You loving that shit, huh?" says Jayvon.

High in his bedroom later, Leon begins packing for Puerto

Rico. He'd "made things right" with Tasha that afternoon, he says, promising her he wouldn't do any more H. What she doesn't know won't hurt her, he thinks, snorting another line.

The next morning, he wakes to the sound of his iPhone alarm—two hours after it started ringing.

"Oh shit," he says, realizing he's overslept. If he leaves now, he thinks, he's got just enough time to pick up Tasha, race to the airport, and check their luggage.

"I'm running late, baby," he tells her by phone, hauling his suitcase out the door. "Can you be outside your crib in five?"

He gets in the car and digs through his jeans pocket, realizing he's still got half a bag of heroin in there. Tasha will kill him if she sees it, so he grabs a notebook lying in his backseat, pours the rest of the powder onto its cover, and snorts it up.

"That's better," he says as the raw kicks in.

A groggy Leon starts the engine and speeds toward Tasha's, nodding off without realizing it.

He's so high, he doesn't feel the bones in his legs, abdomen, neck, and back shatter as his car wraps itself around a utility pole.

It will be weeks before he eats solid food again and months before he walks under his own power.

Six days after Leon's accident, Ronnie Voorhees is packing up her daughter Shandrice's possessions in Philadelphia, wishing she could trade places with her "angel." She comes across some old photos as she works: Shandrice when she was five, her hair done up in ribbon-wrapped pigtails; Shandrice when she was 11, celebrating her birthday at Chuck E. Cheese's; and a third, this one from her college graduation, Shandrice beaming as she crosses the stage to accept her diploma.

"My daughter was a public school teacher, educated at

Temple University, with her own apartment, paid for with her own money," Ronnie says. "But she was also a heroin addict, because where she lived—the gangsters who work here—made her vulnerable."

The drug destroyed her daughter's life so quickly, it "didn't seem possible," Ronnie says. Shandrice, after all, had never so much as smoked marijuana before a BGF set showed up in her neighborhood touting a fresh heroin shipment, her mother says.

"BGF did this to her, just like they've done it to so many others."

BGF's leader in Philly at the time was Timothy "Taye" Braxton, who, at 25, was the same age as Shandrice. She saw him making deliveries on her street in Strawberry Mansion—one of Philadelphia's most drug-saturated neighborhoods—and he saw her staring. They chatted while she walked her chihuahua, Noodle, and quickly hit it off.

Taye was charming, well spoken, and generous with his money, Ronnie says. Soon he and Shandrice were going on dates every other night.

"He told her he was a courier for some office supply company, making deliveries for them, but she must have known better," says Ronnie. "I didn't know anything was wrong, because she sounded happy on the phone every night when we spoke, excited about her work and about meeting someone. Until he started giving her drugs."

Taye was considered a rising star within BGF, so when Pill City launched operations in Baltimore, he was among the first gangsters Lyric called. His Philadelphia set joined the syndicate without hesitation, fellow gangsters say, delivering looted opiates into blighted parts of both Philly and New Jersey while killing a number of rival gangsters throughout the region. By the time Shandrice met him, Taye's franchise had already switched from pill to heroin sales, earning more than $30,000 per week.

But Taye wasn't just selling the stuff. He was using it, too.

"He was shooting 10, 12 bags a day, and he got her started using," Ronnie says. "She told me she was falling in love. I said, 'With who, him or the heroin?'"

Ronnie, who lives in Newark, drove to Philly to try to convince her daughter to enter rehab. But Shandrice refused, insisting she didn't have a drug problem, that she could quit whenever she wanted.

"I begged and begged, did everything but drag her out the door," Ronnie recalls. "And when I left, I knew she wasn't going to stop. Once the heroin takes over, you're finished. My baby girl was finished."

Just a few weeks after her first dinner date with Taye, Shandrice died of a heroin overdose. Her landlord found her lifeless on her bathroom floor, a used syringe stuck in her arm. Toxicology tests revealed the dope in her system was cut with fentanyl.

"Taye used to call it Frankenstein, because it was part H, part fentanyl," Ronnie says. "The police told me it came from Mexico, through Chicago, into Baltimore, then Philly . . . like a deadly migration, just rolling along. But far as I'm concerned, Taye's just as responsible for my daughter's death as those drugs were. I hope he gets his, if not in this life, then the next."

It's not long before Ronnie gets her wish.

In late October, Taye is fatally shot on a drug corner in Strawberry Mansion, a rival Crips dealer putting two slugs through his chest. At his funeral, fellow gangsters praise Taye's "courage" and "heart." They stand over his open casket, muttering tributes, snapping selfies with his corpse—a common mourning ritual among BGF members. Lyric even sends a case of Hennessy cognac to Taye's set, as way of paying his respects.

"I should be glad he's gone," Ronnie says. "But there's so many others selling the same poison, what's the difference?"

Back in Baltimore, still another funeral is being held, this one for Jimmy Masters.

"I swear to God, I'mma handle the niggas who did this," Blackrock says while standing over his father's casket. Patience is seated in the pews behind him, tears streaming down her cheeks. "I swear it."

Though his organization is a shell of its former self, Blackrock refuses to acknowledge defeat. "I got a plan to bring us back," he tells Mondo after the service, the gangsters sharing a blunt in the church courtyard.

"We need more than a plan, yo," Mondo says. "We need product."

"Don't worry, I got both."

Blackrock explains that he had recently gotten a call from Raheem Wallace, a former Masters Organization associate who used to "look after some corners for us down East Side, before he went to college. Boy smart as hell."

Wallace, 37, is a Baltimore native who'd worked his way out of the ghetto, studying computer science at a prominent American university alongside some of the most brilliant minds in programming. A talented hacker and software engineer, he had initially gone to work in Silicon Valley but found he could earn far more selling his services in the underworld. Two years ago, he was released from federal prison following a conviction for orchestrating a lucrative bank hacking scheme. Now he's on the payroll of a Brooklyn-based crime syndicate with ties to the Russian mob.

"He's been stealing data for cloning credit cards, shit like that, but now the Russians . . . they want to move weight, too," Blackrock says.

He continues: "They knew Raheem had some connects in Baltimore, from when he worked for my pop. So they asked him to see what he could do far as distribution goes. He texted me a few days back."

"He still interested?" Mondo says.

Blackrock takes a long pull on the blunt, then lifts a hand to signal a man standing on the edge of the courtyard. The guy takes his time walking over, his eyes hidden by dark sunglasses, a vintage blue Yankees cap tilted sideways on his head.

"Why don't you ask him yourself?" Blackrock says. "Mondo, meet Raheem."

PART IV

TAKING STOCK

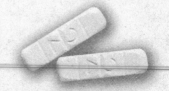

"Murdertown, U.S.A."

I hate this fucking city. I hate it. I hate it. I hate it!

—Mother of Darryl Whitehead, 25, who was killed
by a gunshot wound to the head

West Baltimore

At first, the spate of postriot murders in Baltimore seemed
par for the course—a typical round of springtime killings in a
city long accustomed to violence. On April 28, 2015, Martin
Brooks, 42, was fatally shot on Park Heights Avenue, just
blocks from Pimlico Race Track. The following afternoon,
28-year-old Andre Hunt was killed by a bullet to his head in
Callaway-Garrison. An hour and a half later, and 10 miles
south, Ricky Chambers Jr., 24, was shot to death in Curtis Bay.
Seven hours after *that*, Davon Johnson, 26, was mortally
wounded in Allendale. The next day, 22-year-old James Johnson was blown away by gunfire in Harlem Park.

The five killings happened in the three days immediately
following the Freddie Gray riots, and marked the 72nd, 73rd,
and 74th homicides of the year in Baltimore. Despite the

alarming body count, police leaders weren't yet "in panic mode," says Chris Sheehan, the Baltimore city homicide detective, "but we probably should have been.

"We thought it was an anomaly," Sheehan adds, "that we had three tough days right after the riots, but that . . . things would even out once the city calmed down. Problem was, things didn't calm down. They got worse."

Forty-two people were killed in May, the highest monthly homicide total in Baltimore since August 1990, when crack was still king in the city. June saw 29 more killings. In July, the monthly homicide tally surged to 45, making it the deadliest month since 1972, when Baltimore had nearly 300,000 more residents than it does today.

"Why is this happening?" Davon Johnson's friend, Danika Malone, 23, said after learning her former classmate was murdered. "It's like we got a sickness in this city, and the riots made it spread even faster."

Still, Baltimore's police and government leaders "felt things were bound to improve," Sheehan says. May brought gorgeous weather and, with it, hope for a more peaceful month. Six of the cops involved in Freddie Gray's arrest were arrested May 1, charged with crimes ranging from assault and misconduct to manslaughter and second-degree murder.*

In July, Mayor Stephanie Rawlings-Blake fired the boss of the indicted officers, Police Commissioner Anthony Batts, and promoted his deputy, Kevin Davis, to the top job. Activists and government officials alike applauded the move, characterizing it as a first step toward healing a shaken city.

---

* Three of the officers would be acquitted at trial. Prosecutors later dismissed charges against the other three, acknowledging they stood little chance of winning convictions.

Still, the bloodshed continued. August's punishing heat served as the backdrop for 34 killings, pushing the city's homicide total past that of New York City—an astonishing feat, considering the Big Apple has about 7.8 million more residents than Baltimore. Sheehan and his colleagues "felt overwhelmed" by their caseloads, he says, and Davis soon called on agents from the DEA, FBI, and other federal agencies to help solve the glut of homicides.

"We hoped that in the last three months of the year, we'd start catching up, especially with the feds getting involved," Sheehan says. "But the gangsters kept being gangsters."

Twenty-seven more murders occurred in October; 34 in November; and 31 in December. Police attributed much of the violence to gang-related conflicts over drugs, including looted opiates. As the death toll soared in black communities, families said they felt increasingly powerless.

"My son! Where's my son?" the mother of Darryl Whitehead, 25, cried out on November 4 as she ran toward crime scene tape. Her child lay dead a few feet away, felled by a gunshot to the head. "I hate this fucking city," she howled. "I hate it. I hate it. I hate it!"

By the end of 2015, many others felt the same way.

The city finished the year with 344 homicides, a 63 percent increase over 2014. Per capita, it was the deadliest year in city history, a span that featured rioting, a police slowdown, and a record-breaking influx of stolen narcotics.

"It feels like we're 'Murdertown, U.S.A.,'" Sheehan says.

But Baltimore's homicide tally, frightening as it is, hardly reflects the breadth of the damage inflicted during America's Opiate Wars. Homicides have risen in dozens of other communities across the country, including impoverished swaths of

St. Louis, Washington, DC, Chicago, Milwaukee, Houston, Cleveland, Philadelphia, New Jersey, New Orleans, Cincinnati, Detroit, and Atlanta, records show.

In St. Louis and Chicago, BGF enforcers have lured rival dealers—most of them Bloods or Crips members—into abandoned homes, where they torture them for information before shooting them.

In New Orleans and Atlanta, BGF members have routinely shot up the stash houses and drug corners of enemy crews, killing slingers and customers alike.

In Milwaukee and Cincinnati, Pill City associates have killed 14 rival dealers and civilians combined since May 2015, leading a number of competitors—most of them members of the Bloods and Folk Nation gangs—to relinquish their drug corners. The drug-related violence helped drive up murder rates in a quarter of America's 100 largest cities in 2015—a nearly unprecedented increase.

"The level of violence in inner-city areas where the [opiate] trade is flourishing, and the amount of it we're seeing, has been horrifying," says Marques.

Yet in spite of these tragedies, hope remains, especially among activists.

Word of Booker's and Grier's efforts have spread well beyond Baltimore, inspiring interrupters to launch their own groups across the country. Among them is Darryl Lamb, the Chicago physician who's treated dozens of opiate-addicted babies amid the epidemic's second wave.

"I'm not from Baltimore, but I often feel like we're in a similar situation in Chicago," Lamb says of the addiction and violence plaguing both cities. "It's the kind of kinship I wish we didn't have, but it's undeniable."

Lamb had heard about the addiction interrupters while visiting Baltimore for a medical conference. It was held the same week Jimmy Masters was killed, and word of his death spread quickly through the conference hall.

"Some of these physicians had actually treated [Jimmy's] victims, and many of his employees, for gunshot wounds," Lamb recalls. "In certain circles, including emergency medicine, the guy was very well known."

Lamb left the conference thinking about Julissa Cromartie and her mother, about Masters and his victims, and about all the other dead and wounded connected to the opiate plague's second wave.

"I wanted to do something more to address the problem, and I'd heard about these guys, this reverend and this coach," says Lamb. "They seemed like a good place to start."

He found Grier and Booker's numbers listed online and called them up, peppering them with questions about their activism, keeping each on the line more than an hour.

"I liked their ideas so much, I told them I wanted to start my own [interrupter] chapter in Chicago," Lamb recalls. "All I needed were some folks willing to walk with me."

Whereas Booker relied on word of mouth to recruit interrupters, Lamb recruited his on social media, urging his Facebook, Twitter, and Instagram followers to join him on the streets. On November 2, 2015, the group made its first trek through South Chicago's busiest drug market, an area Calvacca describes as an "open-air bazaar for coke and heroin." Lamb's interrupters endured numerous threats of violence from BGF corner boys and other dealers. But when the gangsters jawed at them, the activists jawed right back.

"Just being out there is enough to mess up their business, and that's exactly what we like to do," says Lamb, who keeps a snapshot of Julissa Cromartie on his iPhone when he goes on patrol—a reminder, he says, of "what's actually at stake out there.

"If we don't fight to save lives in our own communities," the doctor says, "who will?"

"Sky's the Limit"

*We could take our money and go . . . start something
legit in Silicon Valley.*

—Wax

November 8, 2015, East Baltimore

After six and a half months spent atop America's opiate markets, Pill City is finally "coming back to earth," Wax says. The first piece of bad news arrived four days ago, when BGF got wind of a meeting between Philippe Carranza and Raheem Wallace.

Yesterday, Pill City suffered another blow when authorities arrested Slim in Virginia, charging him with first-degree murder in Dome's death.

Today, there's even more trouble: Brick and Wax are working feverishly to fend off a string of hacks targeting Pill City's networks.

"We need to rethink some shit," Wax tells his business partner in their East Side office. "Before things get any worse."

The syndicate's recent troubles have him thinking more about Silicon Valley lately, perhaps even starting a legal business there. To date, Pill City's delivery software and Dark Web drug marketplace have helped facilitate the trafficking of more than $250 million worth of drugs across America, more than Brick and Wax ever thought possible. *Now's* the time to flee Baltimore and find a legal outlet for their talents, Wax thinks, before they both end up in Jessup serving life sentences.

"All I'm saying is, it only takes one nigga running his mouth to ruin everything," Wax says. "Between the heat they're [law enforcement's] putting on us and the [online] security issues, I think we got to start thinking about getting out."

"Man, you ain't even thinking straight," says Brick.

"Nah, man, *you* ain't thinking straight, listening to Lyric too damned much."

Ever since Brick and the BGF set leader started hanging out, Wax hardly sees his best friend anymore. At the same time, Brick's mental health seems to have worsened. He's in his depressive phase at the moment: lethargic, angry, radiating misery. But soon, he's sure to slide over to the "daredevil Brick," Wax thinks, the kingpin who thinks himself indestructible, who craves danger and risk. *That's* the Brick who's been making heroin deliveries with Lyric lately, practically daring the cops to arrest him. During one manic episode, Brick even bought a flashy new car, a BMW 528i with fancy rims and a custom stereo system.

Brick's mood swings don't just make him reckless, Wax believes; they also make him cruel. The last time daredevil Brick reared his head, he had made sure Slim tracked down and murdered Dome, personally instructing him to "make sure it hurt." It reminded Wax of one of their favorite books, *The Godfather*, in which the family's newly empowered patriarch,

Michael Corleone, goes from kind-looking college kid to vi-
cious mafioso seemingly overnight. Michael had done it out of
familial duty, Wax thinks, but Brick's doing it out of sickness.

"Behind every great fortune is a crime," the friends used
to tell each other, referencing *The Godfather*'s epigraph. But
more and more lately, Wax wants to ditch the crime and keep
his fortune—to do something to change his life before it's too
late.

His mother, Brenda Harris, has shown him it's possible.

Two months ago, she'd reached out to Wax following another
relapse, asking if he'd help foot the bill for a rehab stay. Wax
agreed, securing her a spot in one of the most well-respected,
and expensive, treatment centers in the country.

If his mother could make a new path for herself, Wax
thinks, why can't he?

Now, cranking out new code for a security patch, Wax considers his options. Maybe he could launch a small software
company on his own, or get a programming job at an existing
firm in Silicon Valley. With all the money he's made, he never
needs to work again, he knows. But the thing is, he *wants* to.
Coding, design, software engineering, monetizing new technologies: These aren't just hobbies to the teenager; they're his
passions. He'll be 19 next month, and he doesn't want to spend
another year tempting fate.

"I want you to think about it, yo," Wax tells Brick later that
afternoon, both boys chewing on chicken wings while they
work. After their earlier argument, they've settled into a coding groove and, with the help of their hacker friends in Anonymous, appear to have thwarted various attempts to compromise
their networks. "We could take our money and go . . . start
something legit in Silicon Valley. Sky's the limit out there."

"Sky's the limit *here*," Brick says, pointing out the window as the sun sets over West Baltimore. As he does, an emaciated rat scurries under his chair, while in the corner of their work-space, a puddle of putrid water collects on the floor, the home's long-leaking roof still unfixed.

"Sure don't feel like it," Wax says. "Feels like hell to me."

Brick waves his hand dismissively, then, as if in protest, tosses a half-chewed chicken wing across the room. The ro-dent sprints over to the meat, gives it a sniff, and sinks its teeth in.

Quietly as he can, Brick walks over to the animal, raises his booted foot, and brings it down on its head.

"Why you do that?" Wax shouts, repulsed by his partner's cruelty. "Rat ain't done nothing to you."

"He was acting like he owned the damn place," Brick says, lifting his boot to survey his handiwork. The gangster's face is slightly contorted, his eyes glazed over; it is a look that, for the first time, leaves Wax feeling scared of his best friend.

Brick saunters back to his desk, laughing, while Wax hur-ries outside. He hails a cab to his apartment, grabs a duffel bag full of cash from his closet, and takes it to the nearest UPS store, where he ships it to his mother's new address.

Then he heads to the airport.

"I'm done with this bullshit," the kingpin says, just as his plane starts down the runway.

That night, Brick goes looking for his friend.

He tries a number of carry-outs in the area, including Wax's favorite, but the store's empty except for a pair of local rappers locked in a freelance battle, the store clerk serving as judge. One of the contestants, a 19-year-old pill addict nicknamed

Marco the Don, is spitting lyrics about Pill City. Here's part of what Brick remembers he rapped:

> They be gangsters by proxy
> Niggas slangin' that oxy
> Slipping pills to them bitches
> Like they name was Bill Cosby

The other rapper, Quintonio "Qway" McDonald, counters with his own syndicate-related rhyme.

> Shorty need them pills quickly
> Bitch gets 10 pills for 50
> 'Cause Pill City gets money
> Makes they enemies dizzy

Brick's heard about these songs: hip-hop "tributes" that praise Pill City and other drug crews throughout Baltimore. Similar to the Narcocorrido ballads that glorify Mexican drug cartels, they're a way of showing respect for well-known criminals—gangsters with so much money and prestige in the community that their exploits have become part of popular culture. Jimmy and Zeke used to be the subject of such songs. Now it's Brick, Wax, and BGF people are rapping about.

"The songs are kind of funny, but respectful . . . they show Pill City love," Marco the Don tells the carry-out clerk, Ricky Dennis, who's just deemed Marco winner of the freestyle battle. "The ones I like the most are about how you can buy stuff with the pills, trade them for TVs, radios, pussy, anything."

Indeed, Pill City opiates have become a kind of currency

with which addicts can purchase goods and services not just in Baltimore but also in Camden, Cincinnati, Detroit, West Palm Beach, Chicago, and Philadelphia. One 30-milligram oxycodone pill or a $10 heroin baggie typically can be traded for a half hour of sex with addicted prostitutes in many opiate-ravaged, inner-city neighborhoods targeted by the syndicate, authorities say, while a 60-milligram pill or a $20 heroin bag can be swapped for televisions, microwaves, and other goods. But trade away too may possessions, and all an addict is left with is the clothes on his or her back.

"A lot of people out here, they done traded everything for pills . . . they got nothing but themselves to sell," Dennis says.

That's the situation Keisha Jones and Terry Augman find themselves in tonight on Oxy Alley, across town from Wax's favorite carry-out. Both women are injecting roughly $100 worth of pills *and* heroin a day now, funding their habits with a mix of petty theft and prostitution. Keisha's son, Moises, was recently placed in foster care. And Terry, though inching closer to her due date, can't recall the last time she saw a doctor.

"I'm going to see one real soon, though," she says.

The women are holed up in their usual vacant, anxious to take their first heroin injections of the evening. Tony "Deuce" Fenton, a BGF member, delivered the drugs a few minutes ear-lier, warning the women this was a Frankenstein batch, laced with the powerful opiate painkiller fentanyl.

"Don't take too much," Deuce cautioned. "That shit's strong as hell."

But after months of continuous opiate abuse, each woman's tolerance is dangerously high, meaning they must inject more drugs each day to keep pace with "the hunger," as Terry calls her addiction. And it's Terry who, despite Deuce's warning, draws a huge dose of Frankenstein up into her syringe, more heroin than either woman has ever injected at once.

"That's too much," Keisha says just before Terry slams it home.

Within minutes, the pregnant addict's lips are turning blue, her face pale. It's not long before she loses consciousness.

"Breathe!" Keisha shouts to her friend while dialing 911. "Oh God, please breathe."

Forty-five minutes later, Terry is lying on a gurney at Shock Trauma, Dr. Heschel standing over her, searching for a pulse. The doctor tries every tool at her disposal—including Narcan, which the paramedics had also administered—but it's no use. Terry's heart has stopped and won't start again.

Dead, too, is her unborn baby, a female fetus poisoned by the same fentanyl-laced heroin that felled her mom.

"It's not fair," says Heschel, her dark hair grayer now than it was before the riots, the circles under her eyes a little darker.

After noting Terry's time of death, she heads to the women's room just off the ER and lets herself cry: loud, anguished sobs that come from deep inside her chest and last well past her shift's end.

"Civs"

Salvation is at hand, can't you feel it?

—THE REVEREND MARVIN GRIER

November 10, 2015, the Bronx, New York

Wax knocks on his mother's door, holding a bouquet of flowers, his heart beating fast.

"Who is it?"

"It's me, Ma."

Brenda Harris swings the door open, tears streaming down her cheeks.

"I missed you," she says, hugging her son tightly.

Wax can't believe how healthy—how *happy*—his mother looks. She had been at rehab in Delray Beach, Florida, for two months before moving in with her sister in the Bronx. Compared to the last time Wax had seen her, Brenda might as well be a different person.

"Proud of you, Ma," he says. "I guess they were legit."

"Best in the country, hands down," says Brenda.

Wax had been terrified in the moments before his mother

opened the door, fearing she might have already relapsed or gone back to working the streets, just as she'd done every other time she had promised to get clean.

This time seems different, though. Brenda's cheeks look plump and full of color, her frame no longer skeletal like it was when Brick and Wax lived with her. She is clearly in good health, her spirits high.

Now she leads her son inside and serves him two sandwiches: sliced salami on white bread with a touch of mayo, Wax's favorite. They talk all about her time in rehab: the counselors, the addicts, the food, how she'd tried to run away the first week she was there, only to be hauled back in by one of the facility's doctors.

"She was driving to work and saw me wandering in the street like a strung-out fool, knew *exactly* where I'd come from," Brenda says. "She drove me back and that was it . . . I knew I was stuck there until I got clean."

"Was it hard?"

Brenda laughs.

"Hard isn't even the word," she says. "It was the most difficult thing I've done in my life."

Wax knows what that means, coming from his mother. She'd survived years of prostitution, addiction, sexual assaults, and any number of other horrors he'd been too young to comprehend. He pictures his mom in the rehab facility— vomiting, shaking—and thinks about his own customers, the scores of addicts hooked or dead from Pill City opiates. It's not the first time he's considered their plight, but seeing his mother has suddenly reminded him just how damaging the drugs he helps peddle truly are.

Brenda isn't certain of what her son does for a living, but she knows the money he had used to pay for her rehab didn't fall out of the sky. Now she asks him if he's doing anything that might jeopardize his future.

"Not anymore," he says.

"Good," says Brenda. "Because you're too smart to waste your life like I did. I want you to be somebody."

Wax says he'll do his best not to let her down—then shows her the airline tickets he'd recently booked for San Francisco.

"Silicon Valley?" she says. "*That's* my boy."

With Pill City's influence waning, Booker's and Grier's interrupters grow bolder.

Along Oxy Alley, the anti-addiction activists patrol every third night, praying with addicts and dealers, handing out pocket Bibles by the dozen. Near Mount and Edmonson, another interrupter group—this one led by a recovering opiate addict, Otis Washington—spends four hours a day helping people apply for social services. A handful of additional activists personally drive addicts to rehab, the interrupters footing the bill for their treatment—care that can cost an average of $30,000 for a three-week stay.

The money comes from Marvin Grier, who, after being criticized by Slim Robinson for stashing away his illicit earnings, decided to put it toward helping addicts. To date, the funds have allowed more than 30 Baltimore residents to get comprehensive addiction treatment. Grier has plans to help 15 to 20 others in the coming weeks.

"They need the money more than I do," Grier says while driving a pair of heroin users out of Oxy Alley toward an East Side treatment center. "And that young man [Slim] was right on that one issue . . . the money never felt right in my pockets."

The funding has "completely transformed" the way the interrupters go about their work, says Booker, who's been able to purchase hundreds of clean needles and over-the-counter naloxone kits to distribute, along with nutritious meals for hungry and malnourished Baltimore residents.

"Marvin's selflessness is helping us save lives," the coach says, "even though a lot of these folks we approach say they don't want to be saved. That's what addiction does to them, the power it has over the brain. It makes them believe that healing is not in their best interest."

Convincing pill and heroin abusers to get treatment—even when it's free—can be particularly challenging on Oxy Alley, Booker says. Tonight, just two of the 26 opiate addicts approached by interrupters have agreed to enter rehab.* One of them is Tyrone Moxley, a heroin and pill user who had rejected numerous offers for help from the group in the past but "finally broke down and had to make a change" after learning that his ex-girlfriend, Terry Augman, recently died of a heroin overdose, along with his unborn daughter.

"How can I keep living like I been living after that happened?" says Moxley, 26, who'd had little contact with Terry since learning she was pregnant. "Losing her and my child made me see . . . something ain't right in my life."

In the "interrupter van" with Moxley tonight is Kenyata Owens, a 31-year-old heroin addict who's spent the past two and a half years living on the streets, "scrounging up whatever money I could" by collecting recyclables and breaking into

---

* Because of a shortage of program slots at addiction treatment centers throughout Baltimore, most addicts must wait weeks or months for a bed date. The two users in the van tonight are en route to a detox center, but it will be nearly six weeks before they receive comprehensive treatment.

parked cars for pawnable items. Owens overdosed twice on Pill City product in recent months but was rescued both times by Narcan-toting paramedics.

"I done pushed my luck too much already," she says, gazing out the van's windows at all the addicts yet to be saved. "When these men came and offered me help today, I thought, 'Maybe God has a different plan for me.' I'm happy they found me."

The interrupters' efforts, though admired by most, are not without controversy. They've been "cursed at and spit on" by local dealers and addicts, Booker says. A handful of BGF members have threatened them with physical harm, including Lyric and Slim, who's currently in jail on a first-degree murder charge. Authorities say he killed a fellow BGF member, Dome Simmons, for cooperating with the cops. But even behind bars, Slim continues to lobby for Grier's murder, frequently advising Lyric to "touch" the reverend.

Luckily for Grier, Damage has declared him and the other interrupters "civs," BGF shorthand for civilians who are not to be harmed. It's a designation that, based on long-standing BGF tradition, must be observed when declared by a field marshal.

Grier and Booker heard about Damage's gesture and recently sent along their thanks.

"I just hope the peace holds," the coach says.

Two nights later, Lyric dispatches Brick to Damage's home in the suburbs, hoping he can get the field marshal to rescind the civs declaration.

"How," Brick asks his cousin, "can we let them disrespect us like this?"

"They're just trying to help people out, ain't nothing wrong with that," Damage says. "I don't know why y'all are so hung up on this."

Having played ball for Booker, the BGF field marshal admittedly has "a soft spot in my heart" for the coach. But he tells Brick their history played no role in his decision to designate the interrupters as civs.

"Honestly, I think you got shit twisted," Brick insists. "They're costing us money. I got the numbers here to prove it."

Brick pulls a notepad from his pocket and shows Damage the math: In the months since Booker's interrupters took to the streets, Pill City's profits in Baltimore have fallen nearly 20 percent—a loss of more than $3 million. For an organization now forking over hundreds of thousands a week to the Carranzas for premium heroin, the loss is "not something we can ignore," Brick says.

"I think we got to send a message to them niggas," he adds. "I know you don't want the coach touched. But that mothafucker Marvin, he needs to get got."

"Yo, that man's a *reverend*," Damage says. "How you going to touch a reverend without bringing every cop and fed in this city down on us?"

"He ain't a *real* reverend," Brick replies, recalling that Grier was never formally ordained. "He just talks like one. And he's been running his mouth about BGF forever, talking all kinds of shit."

"And you think he should die for that?"

"Hell yeah, he should," says Brick.

Damage looks at his cousin like he's lost his mind, which a lot of people, including Wax, think he has. Damage heard from the Pill City cofounder just this morning, Wax explaining that he'd gone to New York to see his mom and "take a break" from Brick, whose behavior had begun to scare him.

Damage, too, is concerned about his cousin's mental health, wondering how far he's willing to go to silence the interrupters. He tells Brick that, although the activists might be costing the syndicate money, it's "all part of the push and pull of the game," a cycle that dealers and community leaders have been caught in for decades, with few instances of activists being harmed for their efforts.

"There's rules, cuz," Damage says, echoing Zeke Masters's declaration that gangsters, however murderous, must abide by some type of code. "Touching somebody for praying with junkies . . . ain't something that's done."

Brick stares hard at Damage, a menacing look he would have never had the balls to give him a year ago, the older gangster thinks. For the first time, he notices the quality of Brick's new clothes: his Ralph Lauren shirt, Sean John jacket, and $200 pair of Air Jordans. He's been spending wildly in recent months, taking unnecessary risks. Come to think of it, risk seems to be what Brick likes *most* about his work these days. More and more, his behavior reminds Damage of Renata Feeney's: the way she'd "act all types of crazy" when unmedicated, sleeping with strangers, sharing needles, and generally behaving as though she were invincible. Damage recalls his aunt getting involved with Arthur Kane during one of her upswings and using copious amounts of heroin during her downturns.

Now Brick's got the same unhinged look in his eyes, Damage thinks, that his mother had when she was "really up or really down."

"I don't like the way you acting, yo," Damage says. "It ain't you."

"Shit, you think I care?" says Brick, his eyes alight with anger. "I'mma do what I have to do to protect my interests. Lyric, too. Don't matter what you think."

"Oh, that's how it's going to be then," Damage says. "You two all tight and shit now. Best buds."

"After you ran your mouth about Arthur? Yeah, we tight. At least he's loyal."

So that's why his cousin's been spending so much time with Lyric, Damage thinks. The set leader had convinced Brick he couldn't trust Damage, even though Lyric was the one who'd actually been spreading rumors about Kane sexually assaulting Brick.

"I ain't never said nothing like that about you," Damage tells his cousin. "I swear."

"Then how'd Lyric know?"

"Because Arthur used to cop raw from him back in the day," Damage says. "That nigga ain't stupid. He knew Arthur was a sick motherfucker, and he knew you was living under the same roof."

Brick considers the theory for a moment, then brushes it off.

"Regardless of how that shit played out, you still being a bitch about this," he says. "I want [Grier] gone. And that shit's going to happen, one way or another."

"Nigga, this shit ain't your call, Lyric's neither," Damage says. "I'm field marshal, or ain't you forget?"

"Man, *fuck you*," Brick says, storming out of the house.

"Don't do nothing you going to regret, cuz," Damage shouts as he goes.

Alone in his living room later, the field marshal thinks how foolish it would be to kill Grier, imagining the impact such a move would have on Booker. He recalls those long afternoons at practice with the coach, Booker always encouraging him to do better, push harder. He's got "nothing but love" for the man, he says, "even if his business is at odds with ours." Even Grier has "turned out to be a decent dude," Damage says, the former slinger selflessly putting his drug earnings toward helping people get clean.

Out of an abundance of caution, Damage decides to call his cousin before heading to bed, wanting to make clear one last time that Booker, Grier, and the other activists are "off limits, not touchable."

But when he dials Brick's number, his phone goes straight to voicemail.

So does Lyric's.

Please don't let them fools do nothing stupid, Damage thinks.

The Reverend Grier is sitting on a bus bench near Oxy Alley, chatting with a longtime opiate addict about the concept of salvation—whether it has limits, whether it's granted to all who repent—when he sees that same BMW roll past again, its driver's face hidden behind tinted windows. All evening Grier has been walking up and down these blighted blocks, doing outreach work, trying to talk addicts into entering rehab. All evening he has been seeing that same fancy car, as though its driver is watching him, lying in wait.

Whoever it is behind the wheel, Grier doesn't appear worried.

"Those boys ain't stupid enough to come after an old preacher," he says. "I got that much faith in them."

As the BMW's taillights fade into the distance, Grier puts the possibility that he's in danger out of his mind and makes one last plea to the addict on the bench.

"I will pay for every single cent of your care," says the reverend. "You know this is what Cassie would have wanted."

"I know, but today just ain't the day," says Derek Curry, who has known Grier for years. "I do appreciate the offer, sincerely."

They rap for a few more minutes before the one-eyed addict shuffles off into the night, Grier shouting a few final words of encouragement as he goes.

"It wasn't your fault, D. You got to forgive yourself. And Otis, too.

"Salvation is at hand," Grier adds. "Can't you feel it?"

Curry waves and smiles, weighing the reverend's words as he disappears around the corner in search of his next fix.

Grier, undeterred, does another half hour of outreach, walking down blocks bustling with addicts and gangsters, sharing a prayer with anyone willing to stop and talk.

It's just past 11 p.m. when he calls it a night.

"Oof, them doggies are barking," Grier says of his arthritic feet as he drives homes, singing along with the gospel music on his car radio. Enjoying the tunes, he doesn't notice the BMW four car lengths back, its driver making all the same turns as he. Nor does he feel his iPhone vibrating in his pocket, Booker calling to warn him about Brick and Lyric—the coach had just received word from Damage that the reverend might be in danger.

Oblivious to the threat, Grier parks outside his rowhome and heads for the door, whistling one of the last songs he'd heard on the radio, "Amazing Grace."

He doesn't hear the assassin walk up behind him, or see his BMW parked just around the corner, its hood hot to the touch.

"Hey, Rev, got a minute?"

Grier whips around, just as a .38 caliber round blows through his neck.

Afterward, Brick whistles "Amazing Grace" the whole drive home, picking up right where the reverend left off.

"Making a Stand"

The streets are finally talking.

—DETECTIVE JAMAL GRAYSON

"Who," Chris Sheehan says, "would be stupid enough to do this?"

The homicide detective is standing a few feet from Grier's corpse, wondering what it takes for somebody to murder an activist at a time when "every cop in the city is pressing to bring the [homicide] numbers down."

Not only was Grier one of the most respected street preachers in Baltimore, Sheehan says, he'd also been an example of what a man "can accomplish when he reforms himself, chooses a different path for his life.

"In my experience, there's no faster way for a gang to make a community turn against it than by killing someone . . . who's a symbol of good in that community," says Sheehan. "I'm pretty sure the reverend was one of those symbols."

Back at the Western District station, Sheehan's theory is proving correct.

Since news of Grier's death hit the streets, tips about Pill City and BGF have been pouring in: everything from BGF members' birth names and home addresses to vehicle makes and models. The calls to the police tip line are coming in so fast that Grayson, who's volunteered to work the phones tonight, can barely keep up.

"It's like somebody flipped a switch," Grayson says, "and woke people up. The streets are finally talking."

Grier's murder seems to have marked a turning point, he says. Crime witnesses who had formerly been too intimidated to cooperate with law enforcement are speaking up at last, outraged not just by the street preacher's killing but by the breach of protocol that allowed it to happen. Several tell Grayson the "code" Baltimore's gangsters once abided by—the set of rules that typically kept civs safe from harm—was no longer being followed, especially among the city's newest generation of gangsters.

Whatever the tipsters' motives, Grayson says he's happy to finally have some "real leads" to work with in the pill looting probe. He'd been waiting for a break like this ever since the riots, hoping the wave of homicides and opiate overdoses would spur Baltimore's "righteous citizens" to action and help bring Pill City's leaders to justice. Fielding calls, he thinks of all the lives lost since April, beginning with Freddie Gray's in West Baltimore and extending far beyond. The riots carried out in Gray's name were supposed to be a symbol of rebellion, many participants said, an "uprising" meant to get the establishment's attention and signal to police that African Americans would no longer stand for unprovoked violence and racism.

"I think, in some ways, they did get that message across," Grayson says during a break between calls. "But when you look at all the drugs that got put on the streets . . . all the gangsters who took advantage of the situation . . . you have to ask, 'Was it worth it?' In my opinion, given all the lives lost, there's no way it was."

People from all over Maryland come to pay their respects to Marvin Grier: clergy members, cops, Black Lives Matter activists, and, of course, his fellow interrupters. They trade stories about the fallen preacher, marveling at all he'd given this wounded city—his time, his fortune, and, finally, his life.

"He sacrificed all he had to make this city a more peaceful place, a healthier place, a place where every man, woman, and child could live safely and happily, rather than cower in fear," Booker says during the eulogy for his friend. "We have lost a lion of Baltimore."

That evening, at his "homegoing" service, Grier's friends are moved by the memories of his good deeds. They recall his commitment to the community; the long hours he'd spent ministering to addicts; the dozens of men and women he'd personally driven to rehab, paying for the treatment they so desperately needed. But mostly they talk about the colossal void left by his presence; how it can never truly be filled, even by the other interrupters.

And yet, Booker says, they must try.

"He would want us to carry on with his work, regardless of the risks," he tells the mourners.

Later, after the burial, two dozen interrupters gather in the cemetery parking lot, grief-stricken and angry, but inspired, too.

"Now is the time to double down, not pull back," Latonya

Henderson, an interrupter who'd lost a son to heroin-related gang violence, tells the group. "Marvin would want us to keep going."

"She's right," says Otis Washington, the recovering addict whose treatment Grier covered every dollar of and who is now running his own interrupter crew in West Baltimore. "They're trying to scare us off the streets. We got to show them we won't be intimidated."

As the activists talk, more mourners wander over from Grier's grave, joining the conversation. Among them is Jamal Grayson, who has come not just to pay his respects to the reverend, but to see whether any BGF members might be in attendance. Gangsters routinely attend the masses, funerals, and burials of their victims, hoping to intimidate attendees.

But none is brazen enough to show his face here today.

"Welcome, Detective," Booker says, the men familiar with each other through their work with the Police Athletic League. "How you holding up?"

"One day at a time, Coach," says Grayson. "I want to help y'all any way I can."

More funeral-goers walk over, asking Booker how they can help carry on the reverend's mission. Soon there are more than 50 people gathered in the cemetery parking lot, none ready to go home just yet, all wanting to join the cause.

"If y'all are willing," Booker says, "we can get to work right now."

The coach grabs a box of reflective "Life Saver" vests out of his trunk and hands one to each volunteer. He explains the group's mission and methods—the dangers they face, the obstacles they'll likely encounter—then leads a procession of vehicles to Oxy Alley. The activists take to the streets in numbers not seen before Grier's death.

"This is exactly what Marvin wanted, people from all over the community making a stand," Booker tells Grayson as they march down Pennsylvania. "I just wish he didn't have to pass to make this a reality."

The new interrupters chat up every addict in sight, even entering vacants in search of drug users, just like Grier used to do. Over the course of two hours, they convince 11 pill and heroin addicts to enter rehab—a new daily record for the group. A dozen more opiate abusers ask for literature on addiction treatment as well as applications for social services. All agree to meet with Booker the following day for help in filling out the forms.

"Let's keep it going, y'all," Grayson says as they march onto the next drug-saturated street. The detective is smiling, feeling like himself for the first time since Patti's death.

He had even picked up an old friend of his on the way here.

"You heard the man," says Fred Sinclair, linking arms with Grayson. "Let's keep going."

Up ahead, the activists notice a crowd of men standing in the street, 20, maybe 25 guys in all—most of them BGF members. They've come with the intent to intimidate, Grayson knows, but the orange-vested activists don't flinch. They march toward the gangsters, Booker in front, Grayson and Sinclair flanking him on either side. The coach says a prayer as they walk, asking God to shield them from harm and evoking the memory of their slain friend.

"Stand with us, dear Lord, as we walk in the path of our fallen brother," says Booker.

"Amen," shout the marchers, egging Booker on.

"Please, Jesus, help us honor the memory of our friend Marvin by granting us the courage and wisdom and strength to continue his work tonight," Booker says.

"Amen!"

"And allow us, dear Lord, to face the disease in this community head-on, with strength and courage."

Their prayer complete, the interrupters stand face-to-face with a wall of BGF members. Booker spots Damage in the group and gives him a friendly nod, knowing this show of force isn't the ex-fullback's idea.

"What we're here in search of tonight," the coach says, "isn't conflict, it's peace."

"Don't look like y'all here to make peace, far as I can see," says Lyric, the outline of a handgun visible beneath his sweater. "Looks like you coming to send a message and shit."

"Of course we have a message," Booker says. "The message is, we want this community to begin healing. And that starts with you all making sure what happened to our friend Marvin doesn't happen to anyone else."

At the mention of Grier's name, many of the BGF members stare down at the ground, as though ashamed to be associated with the preacher's killing.

Lyric, though, never breaks eye contact with Booker.

"We ain't got nothing to do with what happened to him," the set leader says. "But y'all free to believe whatever you want."

Hearing Lyric lie to the coach's face, Damage decides he's had enough—not just of his set leader's duplicity, but of Pill City's slaying of innocents.

"Y'all free to do your work out here," he tells the interrupters. "And you're right. The reverend ain't deserved that."

Lyric glares at his field marshal with such disdain, Grayson wonders if he might gun him down right there in the street. Damage turns away from the activists, leading his fellow gangsters—all except Lyric—back to BGF's clubhouse.

"Let's go, y'all," Damage says, as Lyric stalks off in the other direction. "We ain't got no beef with these folks."

"God bless you," Booker calls out, proud of his old fullback.

Their path clear, the interrupters march on.

Each night, the group's ranks grow larger: five new members one week, seven the next. Soon a new addiction interrupter chapter crops up on the East Side, followed by another in Washington, DC. As Booker's disciples spread their message on social media, activists around the nation launch similar groups in New Jersey, New Orleans, St. Louis, Kansas City, Philadelphia, L.A., Chicago, South Florida, and other urban areas ravaged by Pill City opiates. One of the most active chapters is Dr. Darryl Lamb's, whose Chicago interrupter group is now 26 members strong and growing.

"We're messing up the slingers' business, helping people get treatment," says Lamb. "People are starting to do this all over [the country]. It's having an impact."

In neighborhoods where interrupters conduct patrols, dealers' profits are diminishing and residents are cooperating with cops in ways few could have anticipated months earlier. Instead of scaring anti-addiction activists and fed-up citizens into submission, it seems Grier's killing has galvanized them.

"Marvin's killer tried to break us," Booker says. "Instead, he empowered communities . . . places that are sick and tired of these drugs."

Thanks to the flurry of tips following Grier's murder, Grayson and his colleagues have arrested numerous BGF members, including Royal Monroe and Deuce Fenton. Grayson says he's close to securing arrest warrants for Lyric and Damage as well.

Amid the surge in arrests, there's new hope among some Baltimore residents that the opiate plague can be beaten back, optimism that the communities targeted by Pill City and their competitors have seen the worst this epidemic has to offer, and persevered.

"I feel like we're winning," Booker says in early December, right around the time Raheem Wallace's street crews start showing up in Baltimore.

The interrupters notice them working Jimmy's old corners in pairs, then, later, in groups of four or five. They dress in black hoodies and jeans, their mouths locked in perpetual scowls. Because of their visibility on the streets, customers flock to them and keep coming back. It turns out their heroin is purer than even Pill City's, and their prices—at $5 a bag versus Pill City's $10—are even more attractive.

At first, no one knows what to make of the interlopers. All BGF knows for sure is that they're calling themselves the Youngstown Boys, or Youngstown Organization, and that one of their senior members is a guy named Raheem Wallace, the same gangster rumored to have met with Philippe Carranza weeks earlier.

Word on the street is Youngstown relies heavily on encryption, using messaging apps like ChatSecure, Adium, and RetroShare to organize its operations. And, like Pill City, they're selling opiates on the Dark Web.

"I don't know where these niggas came from," Lyric says while driving past a Youngstown corner in mid-December. "But they keep this shit up, they going to wish they never stepped foot [in Baltimore]."

PART V

NEW BEGINNINGS

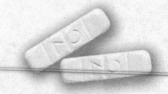

"Clean Money"

We're the better bet.

—Raheem Wallace

December 2015, Baltimore County

"Damn, look who's back from the dead."

The encrypted email from Wax arrives on Brick's nineteenth birthday, the bipolar gangster opening it while still in bed, mired in another depression. The picture of confidence just weeks earlier—strutting, volatile, grandiose—Brick's now an exhausted, paranoid mess, he admits, certain the police will come knocking on his door any moment and arrest him for the murder of Marvin Grier, and maybe even those of Zey and Victoria Walker.

Brick's BGF cohorts are getting scooped up by cops and feds all over Baltimore on gang-related charges, he knows, making it increasingly likely he himself will be captured. On top of all that, he's been having nightmares about Arthur Kane again, the abuser tormenting him even in his dreams.

Seeing Wax's words on his computer screen, though, makes Brick feel a little better.

"Happy birthday," the email says. *"I miss you, yo, regardless of the drama."*

It's been almost two months since Wax fled Baltimore, leaving no hint of his destination. Now he's writing to say he's in Silicon Valley, trying to get a new tech business off the ground. Part of Brick wants to hit "delete" and go back to sleep, and continue living under the assumption their friendship is over. But he can't bring himself to do it, not after all they'd been through together.

"I rented some office space and ordered new gear," Wax writes. *"Not a lot of room to work, but paradise compared to what we're used to."*

Brick rubs the sleep out of his eyes, wondering what it's like to live in California—the sun, the beaches, the girls, so different from the gray, icy streets outside his bedroom window.

"I know you still mad at me, but honestly, I didn't know what else to do. You got to talk to somebody, yo. I've been reading more about bipolar disorder . . . how it's genetic. Ain't nothing you did. It's just something your moms passed on to you. It's not a big deal, if you get medicine for it."

Brick knows his friend is right, that the sickness that helped destroy his mother's life is also destroying his, turning him into someone he can't recognize. He thinks about the lives he's taken—Grier, the Walkers, Arthur Kane. Only Arthur deserved such a fate, he thinks, yet he'd slain them all with the same ruthless efficiency, his disease bringing out aspects of his personality of which he's ashamed.

"Will you please get some help?" Wax writes. *"I love you, bruh. Don't want to see you hurting."*

Brick reads on. He learns Wax is renting a large, two-bedroom apartment in a "safe, quiet, white" neighborhood in the Bay Area—the antithesis of every place they had lived in as children.

"It's a long way from home, but if we succeeded in B'more, we can definitely do it here. Get the same money, but clean money.

"So what I want to know is," the letter concludes, *"you want in?"*

Brick closes the email and surfs the web for a while, reading the *Wall Street Journal* and *Bloomberg* like he did in the old days, imagining what it might be like to go legit, to try his hand at building a "clean" business with his best friend. They had created something unprecedented in Pill City, he knows, a high-tech, drug-dealing juggernaut with no known precedent in America. Couldn't they do the same kind of thing in California, but without having to shed blood or risk prison time?

Maybe we can, Brick thinks, getting out of bed for the first time in two days. *Now that we got the capital, why not?*

He showers, makes himself a bowl of cereal, and goes for a walk around the block, trying to "burn off a little of the haze"—the word Brick uses to describe his depression. Back home that night, he looks up a few psychiatrists online, checking out their websites and patient reviews. Since money's no object, he books an appointment with a well-known doctor in DC, one of the most respected shrinks in the region.

Maybe that's all I need, he thinks. *A little help. Some head pills. A fresh start.*

That night, Brick says a prayer for the first time since he was 10, asking God for mercy, pleading for forgiveness. To his amazement, he sleeps soundly—his slumber devoid of nightmares about Arthur Kane—for the first time in weeks.

"My dad always said, shit ain't over till they close the coffin," Blackrock tells Raheem the following night. "So I appreciate y'all coming through for us like this when we was down."

"Don't even sweat that shit," Raheem says, wearing the black shades that have become his trademark. The computer-savvy gangster's developed a fearsome reputation since returning to Baltimore, routinely ordering his men to carry out killings and stash house robberies, most of them targeting Pill City. Youngstown's been buoyed, too, by the public backlash BGF has faced in the wake of Grier's killing, the preacher's death spurring a number of outraged citizens to cooperate with police against the gang.

"We're in a good position right now, but we ain't done with them niggas," Raheem says.

He's called a meeting of his top lieutenants tonight, including Blackrock, to plan the next phase in their assault on Pill City. The Masters Organization—nearly wiped out by BGF—is now operating under the Youngstown umbrella, as are a number of other local gangs. And all will play a role in the coming offensive against Pill City, Rasheed says.

"Our people in Brooklyn want [Pill City] shut down, so that we can have the whole [Baltimore] market to ourselves."

Pill City's national operations are too big to destroy with guns alone, he explains, but the syndicate's encrypted software and Dark Web marketplace—as well as its heroin and painkiller stashes—are the organization's "weak spots."

"So that's where we going to hit them," he says.

Raheem's plan is simple: Dispatch more Youngstown crews to neighborhoods where Pill City traffics opiates, stake out BGF dealers in those areas, then empty their stash houses of product during gunpoint robberies. At the same time, Raheem says, he'll continue to try to hack the syndicate's encrypted networks, with the goal of introducing a debilitating virus. The two-pronged scheme won't be cheap, he says, but it's being funded by Youngstown's Russian backers in Brooklyn, who'd recently finalized a deal with the Carranzas to purchase Sinaloa-exported heroin.

"The Carranzas changing sides again, huh?" asks Blackrock.

"No doubt, they like winners," says Raheem. "And we're the better bet."

Lyric, sensing that Youngstown is about to make "a serious move," decides to strike first. He dispatches a team of enforcers, led by Damage, to run Raheem's men out of Baltimore.

"Don't fuck this up," he warns his field marshal, the men's relationship having only worsened since Grier's death.

"Ain't much left to fuck up, with the mess y'all already done made," says Damage, who holds Lyric and Brick equally responsible for the preacher's killing, as well as the law enforcement crackdown that followed.

Over the next week, Damage organizes a series of drive-bys and attempted stash house robberies targeting Youngstown, but Raheem's men possess enough firepower to supply a small army: Mac-10s, TEC-9s, Glocks, Berettas, and Lugers, all of which they use to hold off BGF's assaults. Two of Lyric's enforcers are killed and three others injured in the failed offensive, which only serves to embolden Youngstown.

Already reeling, BGF is dealt another blow when Philippe Carranza calls Damage to say he and his brother can no longer supply BGF with heroin: They have a new, better-paying client.

"We're terminating our relationship," Carranza says. "*Lo siento*, my friend. It's nothing personal."

Once word of the Carranzas' deal with Youngstown gets around Baltimore, Pill City's star fades as quickly as it rose. In DC, a team of Youngstown enforcers kills an entire BGF dealing crew over the course of one weekend. In Jersey and Philly, Crips sets aligned with Youngstown raid two major Pill City heroin stashes and run several BGF dealers out of town. Around the same time, Raheem manages to hack into Pill City's encrypted networks, crippling their text-to-delivery service and Dark Web marketplace.

From there, the syndicate's franchises "fall like dominoes," Raheem says. In South Florida, Detroit, Memphis, Milwaukee, Philadelphia, Cincinnati, Atlanta, Staten Island, Chicago, and almost every other area where the organization trafficked opiates, BGF opiate sales cease. By January 2016, Youngstown and their Russian backers are operating in more than 200 inner-city neighborhoods—some just a few blocks long, but still more territory than Pill City held at the height of its power.

"I definitely respect what they accomplished," Raheem says of Brick, Wax, and BGF on New Year's Day, 2016. "But it's our time now."

"Starting Fresh"

We still got time to make things right.

—Wax

Brick, walking in the door after his latest visit to the psychiatrist, decides to start packing up his possessions.

"I'm driving out to Cali *today*, yo," he tells Wax on the phone a little later. "I'm ready to do this thing. Start the new year right."

"That's good to hear, bruh," says Wax, who'd been waiting on Brick's decision. "I'll get the second bedroom set up for you and everything."

Wax can sense the equilibrium in his friend's voice, a result of Brick's first few weeks on lithium and other psychiatric medications. He sounds more like he did before his bipolar disorder spiraled out of control, more like the cool, rational, confident math whiz classmates once called "the Ghetto Stephen Hawking." Youngstown's malicious hacks and stash house robberies have put Pill City permanently out of business, but Brick, who'd been running the tech side of the syndicate on his own since Wax left, doesn't seem the least bit bothered. In fact, he sounds relieved.

"We starting fresh," Brick says. "That's a good thing."

"Plus we still got all that green," Wax says of their illicit earnings.

"Yeah, if I don't spend it all on gas," Brick jokes.

Rather than fly to San Francisco, he's decided to make the 2,817-mile drive from Baltimore in his BMW, viewing the road trip as "a chance to finally travel, see some different things." The partners had once thought their hometown the best place in the world to put their computing expertise to use, its legions of heroin addicts making it the ideal location to launch a tech-driven drug syndicate. But after seeing the horrors their operation inflicted—hundreds of deaths, thousands of newly hooked addicts across the United States—both say they wish they had never started Pill City.

"We can't change what's done, I guess," says Brick, whose trips to the psychiatrist have been supplemented with daily treks to church for prayer services.

"But we young," says Wax. "We still got time to make things right."

"Make *some* things right, maybe," says Brick, who doesn't think God will forgive him for the murders he's committed or the drug deals he's helped facilitate. He places himself in the same category as Arthur Kane: "Irredeemable," he says.

"Arthur did what he did to me, and I did what I did," Brick says. "It's a cycle. That's what my doc's been telling me."

"Maybe, but out here, you going to put all that mess behind you," Wax says. "No more drama."

Brick's on the road 20 minutes later, driving west, hoping his friend is right.

The deal Lyric cuts with Raheem is simple but risky.

Youngstown's leader has commissioned him to murder both Brick and Damage—the only gangsters Raheem still views as a threat in Baltimore. In return, Lyric will get a "place at the table" in Raheem's gang, he says, including a cut of their drug earnings.

"You can't control them [Brick and Damage], so they got to go," Raheem says, the gang leaders meeting outside a busy seafood restaurant in Mondawmin to finalize their deal. "Damage ain't loyal, and the other boy still got the skills to put them back in business . . . tool up and make another move on us."

"When you want this done?" says Lyric, who doesn't seem bothered by the undertaking. After all, he's wanted Damage dead since the day he took over as set leader, he says, and considers Brick a "mental case" who "got so messed up from Arthur raping him, his mind ain't been right since."

"When I want this done?" Raheem says, incredulous. "I want it done today, nigga, when else? Those boys both probably fitting to leave town right about now, if they haven't already."

Under normal conditions, Lyric thinks, he might put a bullet in someone's head for talking to him like that. But he's placating Raheem as a "means to an end," he admits to this reporter, hoping to ingratiate himself with the Russians in Brooklyn and eventually to displace Raheem as Youngstown's leader.

After the gangsters part ways, Lyric climbs into his SUV, loads a fresh clip into his 92FS Berretta, and starts out for Brick's apartment, getting there just as his target's pulling out of his parking spot.

"Right on time," he says.

"Loose Ends"

Closed casket for that ass.

—Damage

January 2016, Southern Pennsylvania

Brick drives more than two hours before stopping, Lyric tailing him at a safe distance, careful not to get made. He exits the interstate somewhere in southern Pennsylvania, pulling into a gas station to fill up.

"Long trip ahead of me," he tells the station attendant, placing a few candy bars and premade sandwiches on the counter.

"You picked a good night for it," the attendant says. "Weather couldn't be nicer."

It's a clear, crisp evening, and Brick is admiring the moon and stars as he pumps fuel, wondering, perhaps, what lies in store for him on the West Coast. In his BMW later, authorities will find a handwritten list of things he'd planned to do in the Bay Area: tours of Google and Apple, an afternoon at a Giants game, even a meeting with an investor whom Wax thought might be willing to offer seed money for their prospective new business: a high-tech, fully legal marijuana delivery service, with operations in Washington, Colorado, and Oregon.

But Brick, hopeful as he is, never gets beyond the gas station. His tank is just about full when the 9-millimeter round enters his brain, Lyric firing from point-blank range.

As Brick's closest relative in Baltimore, Damage gets a visit from the cops that night, informing him of his cousin's murder. They ask him if Brick was involved in drug trafficking—whether anyone might have had a reason to target him. They show him a picture of the shooter's SUV, taken from a surveillance camera in Pennsylvania.

"James was an innocent . . . I can't think of one person who wanted to hurt him," Damage lies. In truth, he'd immediately recognized the vehicle as Lyric's, and knows with certainty it's the set leader who had slain his cousin. "I don't know who'd do something like that."

When the investigators leave, Damage retrieves a shotgun from his bedroom closet, pulls up a chair by the window, and waits for his boss.

"Lyric trying to tie up loose ends," he says. "Guess I'm one."

The BGF set leader blasts his stereo all the way back to Baltimore, a little Nas, a little Biggie, anything to pump himself up for the killing still to come. Midnight finds him parked outside his field marshal's house in the suburbs, loading a fresh clip into another gun, this one a Glock 43 with its serial number scratched off. He takes a few deep breaths, steeling himself for the task at hand, then exits the SUV.

He's preparing to sneak around back, maybe break in through a window, when Damage's front door swings open.

"Thought you'd a been here sooner, boss," the homeowner says, his Remington 870 trained on Lyric's midsection.

The first blast penetrates the set leader's abdomen; the second puts him on his back. He gurgles a few, indecipherable words before going quiet.

For good measure, Damage trains his gun barrel on the dying gangster's face, squeezing off a final slug.

"Closed casket for that ass," he says.

A neighbor hears the gunfire and calls 911, but Damage, moving swiftly, peels out of his driveway before officers arrive. He calls Booker a few minutes later.

"I need a place to go, Coach," Damage says. "Something I did."

He gets to Booker's just after 1 a.m., the coach inviting him in without question, fixing him a plate of meat loaf and mashed potatoes—a final meal, it's understood, before Damage turns himself in.

"You going to be all right, son," the coach says.

They talk for two hours, about football and food, the weather and women, anything to delay the inevitable.

Finally, with Damage's approval, Booker calls 911.

As the first of many patrol cars turn down his street, the coach hurries into his bedroom, returning with a small gold crucifix.

"It was my baby girl's," he says, handing the charm to his old fullback, embracing him as the first officers enter. "Take it with you and try to remember: Out of bad things, good things come."

Grayson, too, is trying to keep the coach's axiom in mind. A week or so after Damage's arrest, the detective exits his Delta flight in California, nervously awaiting a reunion with his sons. He hasn't seen them in four years, a gap of which Grayson says he's ashamed but hopes to make up for starting today. He wonders if Nate and Charles will remember him, whether they'll be able to recognize him after all this time.

"Truth be told, I'm hoping I can recognize them, too," he says, hauling his suitcase through the air bridge. "A father should never have to say that, but there it is."

He considers all that's happened the past few weeks: Grier's murder, Pill City's collapse, Youngstown's rise, and the deaths or arrests of multiple BGF members. The pharmacy lootings probe is stalled,* he says, the identity of Pill City's founders still a mystery. But Grayson's got a different assignment these days: the Youngstown Boys are now his primary target.

He still hasn't forgiven himself for Patti's overdose, he says, but he's "getting there," thanks in part to the friendships he's forged with other narcotics investigators this past year, especially Marques and Calvacca.

"What we all talk about . . . what we've all learned from this case is, you've got to separate your work from your personal life, or it will kill you," Grayson says. "I'm trying to get better at that."

Entering the terminal, Grayson looks to his left and right, scanning the crowd for his sons, both of whom are in their teens now. Then, directly ahead, he sees a cardboard sign: "Welcome to L.A., Detective Dad." On either side of it are Nate and Charles, both tall and broad-shouldered, both the spitting images of their father. Grayson rushes over, kissing each boy on the top of his head.

"I love you," he says, and both of his sons say it back, without hesitation.

---

* As of this writing, just two people have been convicted on charges connected to the April 2015 pharmacy lootings. The investigation remains active, and authorities have said they are still searching for as many as 70 suspects.

"Brave Folks"

A man's got to start somewhere.

—Derek Curry

The interrupter van is packed today. Otis Washington is at the wheel, Coach Booker beside him. Seated in the back are three men and one woman, all addicted to either heroin or painkillers, all former Pill City customers who, in recent weeks, have been getting their drugs from Youngstown.

"Y'all some brave folks," Otis says, decked out in new jeans and an orange interrupter vest—a far cry from the flickering-eyed, hopeless-looking addict Grier had stumbled upon in an Oxy Alley vacant last year. Otis recently got a part-time job at Safeway and devotes the rest of his time to interrupter outreach work and attending addiction support groups.

"I know what you're going through at this moment," he tells the addicts in the van. "All I can say without a doubt is, you're doing the right thing. Because after today, everything changes."

Otis has played a crucial role in the organization since Grier's death. Booker put the ex-sanitation worker in charge of "addict outreach," volunteer recruitment, and various other programs. The coach needs all the help he can get these days, he says, now that his group consists of nearly 70 members. To date, the activists have helped more than 100 opiate abusers across the region enter rehab—all of their treatment paid for with money Grier left Booker in his will.

"We've helped quite a few people," Booker says. "But we've still got a lot of work ahead of us."

The Baltimore interrupters, as well as those in Chicago, St. Louis, and Camden, have begun purchasing used buses and vans, building a fleet with which to drive addicts to rehab. They've also received seven donated vehicles, with more being offered every week.

"People realize this is a grassroots effort to combat addiction, and at the grassroots level, everyone in the community needs to chip in," Otis says. "This is how we're going to beat this thing, by coming together in our communities to help our sick brothers and sisters."

Booker looks back to check on the addicts and sees one of them, a pretty young woman, crying into her shirtsleeve. He asks her if she's all right.

"Yeah, I'm just missing my son a lot right now," she says.

Later, outside the rehab center, she introduces herself to the coach.

"My name's Keisha Jones," she says. "I just want to thank you. I know how expensive this is."

"Don't even mention it," Booker says, thinking he recognizes the woman from his many patrols on Oxy Alley. She starts to cry again, trembling for want of opiates. "You're going to get better in there. You know that, don't you?"

"I hope so," she says. "For his sake."

She pulls a faded photograph from her purse, a shot of her smiling son, Moises, just after he'd turned five. She'd snapped it before the riots, back when she'd still had a steady job, before she and Terry started wondering what those Pill City boys were all about.

"What a happy little boy," says Booker, admiring the picture. "Do you want him back?"

"More than anything," Keisha says.

"Then go make it happen," the coach says, his talent for motivating coming in handy yet again, but far from the gridiron this time.

At that, Keisha bounds into the clinic, deciding that, whatever happens behind these doors, she's coming out clean.

Otis, figuring he'll make one last pass of Oxy Alley, turns down a block he hasn't patrolled in a while. It's a blighted stretch of blacktop once dominated by BGF, but Youngstown dealers now hold sway there, clutching smartphones and heroin baggies, peddling drugs as though nothing's changed.

"Same drugs, new faces," Otis says, lamenting the neighborhood's deterioration.

Amid the smattering of slingers and addicts, he spots his old friend Derek Curry. The men haven't spoken in years—not since the day Curry attacked him, enraged over the Oxy-Contin he had sold to Curry's wife. At the time, Otis had no idea how potent the painkillers were, having just procured them from one of Jimmy Masters's dealers. But soon everyone in Baltimore would know about OxyContin, for the drug left hundreds dead across the region starting in the late 1990s.

Otis, summoning his courage, rolls down his window to give Curry a nod. He's surprised by how much the ex-guitarist has aged, his once-thick hair reduced to a handful of gray patches, and his hands—the tools that made him one of the finest musicians in Baltimore—now raw with sores and burns.

"Otis? God bless, I thought you was dead, man," says Curry. "How long you been clean?"

"Couple of months," says Otis. "Taking it one day at a time, you know how it is."

Curry walks over, trying to calculate how many years it's been since their fight. At least a dozen, he thinks, maybe more. Neither man can remember with certainty, the drugs they took having claimed too many memories, both good and bad.

"Eye's still gone, as you can see," Curry says with a laugh, pointing at his patch.

"You know, I never apologized," says Otis. "I should have."

The recovering addict recalls the details of their fight— Curry swinging on him without warning, Otis defending himself a little too well, bloodying the musician's face with a barrage of punches.

"Me, too, man," Curry says. "But listen, that's water under the bridge."

They bump fists, as if making their truce official. As they do, a Youngstown dealer swaggers over, asking Curry if he needs some dope.

"Nah, I'm good, yo," he says.

When they're alone again, Otis asks Curry if he's thinking about "cleaning up."

"Only if y'all still willing to pay for it," Curry says.

"Of course we're willing," Otis says, wishing Grier were there. "Comes courtesy of the good reverend."

Curry recalls the last time he saw the preacher, a half hour or so before his death. Grier had been trying to convince Curry to enter rehab that night, insisting it was time to forgive himself—and Otis—for Cassie's death.

Maybe, Curry thinks, it really *is* time.

"A man's got to start somewhere," he says, climbing into the interrupter van.

"Trapped"

Everybody beefing in here, all of them thinking they in the right, that they the chosen ones.

—DAMAGE

January 25, 2016, West Baltimore

Damage is sitting in his jail cell, clutching the crucifix his former coach gave him—the charm that once belonged to Brittany Booker. The field marshal's never been a religious man, but he says the gift is meaningful nonetheless. It's the one item he'd successfully smuggled into the detention center, his one keepsake from life before incarceration.

"I've been going to the inmate [church service] they got here every Sunday, seeing what it's about," says Damage, fresh off his weekly visit from Coach Booker. "I wouldn't say I had a religious awakening or nothing like that, but I feel something real when I pray, no doubt."

Three cells down from Damage's is that of his old nemesis, Slim Robinson, the dispute between the gangsters having ebbed now that both are behind bars. Inside, they've got mutual enemies: Bloods, Crips, Highlandtown Soldiers,

Youngstown Boys, and members of dozens of additional crews. Gangsters like Damage and Slim are marked men these days, with Youngstown offering a $2,000 bounty on the head of every Pill City associate still in Baltimore.

There are plenty of potential takers out there, now that eight area gangs are working in league with Youngstown, creating the kind of supercartel Jimmy Masters once envisioned.

"It's like the Royal Rumble in this bitch, every *type* of gangster," Slim tells Damage one afternoon in the jail library, the men discussing life on the outside versus in detention. "Out there, we had to worry about all these mothafuckers, but not under the same roof as us."

"For real, can't rest for a minute even," Damage says, flipping through a copy of the Old Testament, thinking how similar things were back then to the way they are today. "Everybody beefing in here, all of them thinking they in the right, that they the chosen ones. But they got to realize, we all in the same boat. We *all* trapped."

The gangsters, both awaiting trial for murder, say they wish they'd made different choices on the outside: Damage that he'd stuck with football and steered clear of gang life; Slim that he'd stayed in the Army and "took whatever these bad impulses are in me and . . . did something useful with them."

Neither man expects to taste freedom before middle age.

"Maybe one day," says Slim, flipping open a Bible of his own, "we'll be like Reverend Grier and them, all righteous and shit.

"Nigga wasn't scared of nobody," he adds. "Even us."

"Best City in the World"

I've worked in places a whole lot rougher than this.

—W<small>AX</small>

"You know, he doesn't *look* like a drug dealer," the guy two cubicles from Wax's says.

"That's because he's a programmer, for Christ's sake," says a girl sitting across the room. "Don't be so racist."

"I'm just saying, that's the rumor."

Wax is in the office's downstairs bathroom, giving his colleagues a chance to discuss how this potbellied, eyeglass-wearing 19-year-old—the only black person in the whole place—managed to land a job at one of the hottest tech start-ups in town. William Harris, as he's officially known, is beginning his third day as a programmer with the firm, a job with excellent pay, good benefits, and, most appealingly to Wax, the chance to design groundbreaking software.

Working there wasn't the teen's first choice—he'd have much rather launched the legalized weed delivery service he'd dreamed up with Brick—but it felt wrong pursuing the business without his best friend. *Everything* felt wrong without Brick, in fact. In his grief, Wax felt the best thing was to get back to coding; to try to stay busy and keep his mind off his best friend's murder.

At his new job, he's been dubbed the "nerdy-looking black guy" from Baltimore, the kid with the 2016 Jaguar F-Type convertible who blasts hip-hop in the office parking lot. There are rumors he sells drugs, that he's been to jail, even that he's on the run from the law. But Wax just laughs off the gossip. As far as he's concerned, the only person whose opinion matters in this place is the CEO, who'd taken one look at Wax's software portfolio—the Pill City program *not* among his work samples—and hired him on the spot.

"What's up, y'all?" Wax says, returning to his cubicle, eyeing the crowd of gossipers nearby.

The group scurries back to their desks, looking embarrassed. But one of them, the girl who'd defended Wax, flashes a smile.

"Crazy that we don't have bathrooms on our floor, huh?" she says.

"To be honest, I don't really mind," Wax says, thinking of his and Brick's old office, the leaky, rat-infested vacant where they'd helped facilitate more than a quarter billion dollars in drug transactions. "I've worked in places a whole lot rougher than this."

The girl laughs. She is twenty-something, Asian, long brown hair. Beautiful, Wax thinks. She has a Princeton University pennant on her cubicle wall; says her name is Lisa Wu.

"Hey, have you taken your break yet?" Lisa asks. "If not, I know a great sandwich place that just opened."

"Yeah, I'm starving," says Wax. "Want me to drive?"

They're zooming down the freeway five minutes later, the top open in Wax's Jaguar, Lisa's hair blowing 10 different ways. Wax is singing along to the song on the radio, Kendrick Lamar's "Alright," feeling the best he's felt since that day on the shooting gallery stoop, the day he'd devoured Iceberg Slim's autobiography with his new best friend.

"So, what kind of work did you do before this?" Lisa says.

"Coding, mostly," says Wax.

"Me too," Lisa says, shading her eyes with her hand, the afternoon sun beating down on both of them, the sky a cloudless stretch of blue.

Wax thinks about how much Brick would have liked it here—the sun, the girls, the money—and how close he'd come to making the journey. He recalls his best friend's funeral in West Baltimore, the service reminding him so much of Renata Feeney's: sparsely attended, solemn, a vague air of inevitability permeating the affair.

He realizes now that they had been doomed by their surroundings—violence, poverty, abuse, and addiction all too much to overcome. But Wax also knows it's the city that made him strong, that made two boys from the hood believe anything was possible.

"Did you like living in Baltimore?" Lisa asks a little later. "I only know it from what I saw on TV, during the riots."

It's the one question Wax doesn't have to think about.

"B'More?" he says. "It's the best city in the world."

Afterword: "A Marshall Plan for Addiction"

Capitalism is great for a lot of things, but not for heal-ing addiction.

—DARLA MCGOVERN

March 2016, West Baltimore

With high-tech gangs like the Youngstown Boys creating a new generation of addicts, America's opiate epidemic is spiral-ing further out of control. Nearly 30,000 people die from pain-killers and heroin annually. Thousands more are brought back from the brink of death with naloxone. And people in every zip code find themselves in thrall to the morphine molecule, hundreds of new addicts joining their ranks each day.

This scourge is affecting black and white, rich and poor, inner cities and suburbs alike. It can still be beaten back, ex-perts say, but it won't be easy. The effort will require billions of dollars in federal, state, and local funds distributed *fairly* among minority and white communities; comprehensive, fully funded legislation in Washington, DC, to address the opiate crisis; a major expansion in the coverage and availability of treatment; and an unprecedented effort by families, nonprofits, and activists like Booker and Lamb to heal drug-ravaged communities.

If that sounds like a major undertaking, consider the alternatives: between 25,000 and 35,000 Americans dead from opiates each year for the foreseeable future; the continued, relentless flow of dope, fentanyl, and painkillers into poor, racially isolated neighborhoods; and the ever-growing influence of sophisticated drug crews—organizations that rely on encryption and connections to Mexican drug cartels to blanket this nation with opiates.

"What we need," says Dr. Heschel, the emergency room physician at Shock Trauma hospital, "is a Marshall Plan for Addiction. Not baby steps, not incremental legislation or piecemeal solutions, but a massive, sustained, serious effort all across this country dedicated to ending this epidemic everywhere, including communities of color."

The first step in such an effort, experts say, should be a massive increase in federal spending on treatment and prevention. Not next year, but *today*.

"It's imperative the government devotes more money to fighting the nationwide opiate epidemic right now—in poorer, underserved communities as well as more affluent ones—because what they're spending isn't nearly enough, and more people are dying every day," says Brian Dufresne, a former CDC researcher who advises patient advocacy organizations. "New expenditures in the hundreds of millions isn't going to cut it, not when you've got drug gangs consciously targeting disenfranchised citizens and enough Mexican heroin coming into this country to keep every American high in perpetuity.

"Another tragedy is, we've got entire minority neighborhoods being left to combat this epidemic almost wholly on their own," Dufresne adds. "It's not right, and I don't think it's who we want to be as a country. Our message to Washington is: Help these folks get better."

Congress seems to have grasped the scope of the problem, yet still isn't doing enough. In July, lawmakers passed the Comprehensive Addiction and Recovery Act—the first major federal addiction legislation in 40 years—but they included just a fraction of the funding needed for new treatment programs.

With Donald Trump's surprise election victory in November 2016—and Republicans holding majorities in both chambers of Congress—it's unclear what additional steps the federal government will take to combat the opiate crisis in 2017, if any.

The government is poised at the time of this writing to spend less than $200 million in the coming months on an epidemic that kills far more Americans each year than terrorism, Ebola, and AIDS combined—yet receives less funding than each of these.

That dollar amount "is far too small when you consider the scope of this problem," says Rhodes, who lost a close friend and colleague to a prescription opiate overdose in September 2015. She says she applauds the CDC's recent change to prescribing guidelines, which urge doctors not to prescribe opiates for chronic pain.

"But we need more than just guidelines," Rhodes adds. "We need to be talking about dollar amounts in the 10 to 15 billion [dollar] range if we're going to start turning back the tide."

One doctor at Johns Hopkins Bayview Medical Center in Baltimore says the federal government should take Dr. Heschel's advice and fund something "on the order of" the Marshall Plan—the U.S. aid package that provided nearly $13 billion in funding (about $130 billion in today's dollars) to help Europe rebuild after World War II.

"That's how big we need to be thinking, if we want to see

the end of this epidemic in our lifetimes," this doctor says. "If we declare war on opiate addiction, and that's the drug war we *should* be fighting, we can fund treatment for every addicted man, women, and teenager in this country. And it makes economic sense, too. Do you have any idea how much more productive a society we'd be if we turned those folks back into healthy, productive members of the work force?"

In addition to increasing funding, there are concrete steps the government can immediately take to save users' lives, authorities say. First, public health officials and lawmakers can expand access to methadone and Suboxone, maintenance therapies that cut the chance of fatal overdose by half. They also can do away with regulation that caps the number of patients a single doctor can treat with Suboxone and makes the drug impossible to procure in many parts of the country. In July 2016, the Department of Health and Human Services raised the limit on how many patients a doctor can treat with the drug at any given time from 100 to 275. But critics say that's still too low.

"Effective as methadone and Suboxone are, they continue to carry a stigma among certain medical practitioners, simply because they contain opiates," says the Johns Hopkins physician. "And that stigma has led to regulations that are doing more harm than good, cutting off access to treatment for addicts who, sooner or later, will end up dead without that help."

Ninety percent of U.S. counties have no methadone clinic or possess supplies of the drug that fall far short of demand, according to research by the RAND Corporation. And because of federal restrictions, 43 percent of U.S. counties don't have enough Suboxone prescribers to meet demand. (Many municipalities have no Suboxone prescribers at all.)

It's a painful irony: As of June 2016, more than 900,000 U.S.

doctors could write prescriptions for opiate painkillers like OxyContin, Percocet, and Vicodin, but, because of federal rules, fewer than 32,000 physicians could prescribe Suboxone, according to research by the Pew Charitable Trusts.

"As long as that . . . gap exists," Heschel says, "we will not end this epidemic."

The DEA, too, can slow the rate of opiate deaths, simply by reducing the number of prescription opiates drug makers are permitted to manufacture. Such a move would ensure there are enough pills in circulation for those who need them but not the surplus of painkillers that exists today.

During the presidential campaign, Trump called for a reduction in opiate production, citing research that shows the United States has 5 percent of the world's population but uses 80 percent of its prescription opiates. Trump also said he wants to increase the number of patients who doctors can treat with Suboxone, and promised to slow the flow of heroin and fentanyl into America by securing the nation's borders.

Whatever actions the new administration takes, government oversight ought to play a bigger role in fighting the epidemic; Lawmakers should hold insurance companies accountable for the way they're "mistreating" opiate addicts and their families, denying addicts quality treatment in their time of need, says Rhodes.

Despite the Affordable Care Act's mandating coverage for addiction treatment, insurers continue to place onerous restrictions on opiate abusers seeking help, often requiring that they "fail out" of an outpatient treatment program before inpatient treatment can be approved. Even then, many insurance companies approve just a few days of treatment at a time, limiting the amount of care patients receive. As a result, thousands of Americans are forced to haggle with bureaucrats even as their sons, daughters, husbands, and wives suffer from life-threatening addiction.

The numbers demonstrate the scope of the problem: Just 11 percent of Americans in need of addiction treatment actually receive it, due to a shortage of program slots and skyrocketing health care costs. Inpatient rehab stays can cost between $20,000 and $60,000 a month, an amount that's out of reach for many families. Those who do enter rehab still face long odds, with as many as 60 percent of heroin users relapsing within a year.

Part of the problem is a lack of resources. Local, state, and federal funding has not kept pace with the increase in new opiate addicts, especially in poorer, minority neighborhoods. Less funding means that fewer addiction counselors and doctors are hired, which means longer wait times, fewer beds, and more addicts denied treatment. The penny-pinching exhibited by insurers, authorities say, is only making things worse.

"We know there are fewer treatment options available to the poor and disenfranchised, and that's an imbalance we should all be ashamed of," Heschel says.

The disparities in treatment for rich and poor are glaring in other ways, too.

Top-of-the-line rehab centers—expensive clinics with the most experienced doctors, best-trained counselors, and most opulent facilities—tend to cater to a wealthier, whiter clientele, customers with top-of-the line insurance and enough money to fund their stays indefinitely. Such facilities can take on the feel of a "country club," says the Hopkins doctor, "while back in the ghetto, your typical rehab center is underfunded, dingy, dark, and depressing . . . not the kind of place you really want to be when you're craving a shot [of opiates]."

One of these "dark, depressing" facilities is the Green Willow South treatment center, located in a crime-ridden, impoverished section of Bridgeport, Connecticut. Here, in urine-scented rooms crowded with detoxing patients and frazzled care providers, opiate addicts are treated with outdated equipment—the result of years of budget cuts at all levels of government. Many of the clinic's staffers earn poverty wages; in some cases, even less than the wages of the poor patients they treat.

These employees say the private rehabilitation system in general is designed to siphon money from everyone involved— "the workers, the patients, the insurance companies, the government, everyone except the folks who own these places and use them to get wealthy, just like any other business owner," says Darla McGovern, an addiction counselor at Green Willow, who has worked at five different rehab facilities in her 20-year career.

"Capitalism is great for a lot of things, but not for healing addiction," she adds. "It just keeps people broke *and* addicted."

As for government-funded rehab, centers like Green Willow can be even worse than privately owned facilities. Jonathan Underwood, a 47-year-old auto mechanic who has done six monthlong rehab stints at "the Willow," as regulars call it, says that in "places like this [and he has been at several], we're almost all black or brown, which means the funding [the facilities get] is always going to be less than in the white part of town. We know that . . . we're used to it."

Today, Underwood's talking to a newly hired addiction counselor, Joy Matthews, also a recovering opiate addict, about Underwood's "love affair" with the ritual of injecting heroin, specifically the black tar variety. Injecting opiates has left

Underwood's body covered in wounds. But that hasn't stopped him from shooting up each day for the past 14 years.

"What I do is, I put the little chunk of dope on my spoon and soften it up a little with water from my rig," Underwood explains, his voice slowing as he speaks, as if describing the ritual alone is enough to get him high. "I cook the dope up with the lighter, get it bubbling, till she's melted down. Once I get a vein I think will work, I ease the rig in, pull back [on the plunger], and wait for the flag."

The "flag," or "red flag," as it's known to intravenous opiate users the world over, is the trickle of blood that floods into the syringe once the plunger is pulled, signaling that "you're in business, that you got a good vein and you about to get high," Underwood says.

Like scores of addicts, he's become addicted to the sight of the red flag, he says, associating "the bloody little cloud" with the feeling of the needle breaking through his skin and that first, blissful wave of opiates coursing through his bloodstream.

"Many times over the years, if I didn't have no heroin or pills, I'd heat up some tap water and inject that by itself," says Underwood. "I'd get high just seeing the flag and feeling the rig under my skin. It's not as good as the real thing, but it's still damned good. That's what I mean by love affair . . . everything about [using] is like being in love, and you think the dope loves you back, but it don't."

"Don't I know it," Matthews tells him, later recounting her own battle with addiction. The counselor became hooked on painkillers after purchasing OxyContin and Vicodin on a Bridgeport street corner in 2010. Soon, swallowing the pills "stopped doing the job," McGovern says, "so I started shooting them instead.

"I was broke from spending all my money on pills, so I had

to use the same needle over and over," she recalls. "I was using these really dull rigs, hardly any point on them at all, just jabbing myself all over until I got a vein that took. And, you know, sometimes I'd just be shooting a little dust, like what was left over from the last pill, crawling around on the floor picking up specks that I'd spilled.

"But I still loved seeing the flag, seeing the blood flow up in there like . . . something really amazing was about to happen when I pushed it all back in. After a few months, looking in the mirror . . . seeing what all those dull rigs did to me, I was like, damn . . . I knew I had to stop."

Once their session is over, Matthews logs into her computer to make notes on Underwood's progress. But the machine—a Dell desktop from the early 2000s—crashes before she can complete the task. A few minutes later, Matthews's supervisor, Regina Carpenter, is forced to close the facility down for the day after a gang-related shoot-out between drug dealers erupts on the sidewalk outside.

"We do whatever we can for these folks, but it's sad," Carpenter says, eyeing the police cars across the street. "As a country, we've got to take care of each other. We've got to do this thing together, black, white, broke, rich, everyone.

"Or else," she adds, "the dying's never going to stop."

About This Project

My reporting for this book began on April 27, 2015, when an underworld source of mine—a former Bloods gang member from Long Island, New York—texted me these words: "Shit's going down in B'more, son. Get down here soon as you can."

The text was from Clarence "Cuddy" Moss, one of the toughest, smartest gang members I have ever covered. For four years, from 2008 to 2012, Cuddy helped oversee a multimillion-dollar drug racket in New York City and its suburbs, trafficking heroin and cocaine through parts of Queens, Brooklyn, the Bronx and Westchester, Nassau, and Suffolk Counties. Merciless as he was calculating, Cuddy personally shot at least five men during his gangland career and ordered the murders of several others. But each time prosecutors sought witnesses to his crimes, the social prohibition against snitching—so pervasive in gang-plagued neighborhoods—derailed their cases.

His knack for staying out of prison earned Cuddy the nickname "Teflon Don," since, like his Mafioso predecessor John Gotti, he always found a way to wiggle out of legal trouble. For a while, it truly seemed he was invincible—immune not just from legal repercussions, but from gangland retribution.

Then the Crips came after his family.

The first relative they got to was Cuddy's stepbrother, Samuel, a 20-year-old restaurant busboy living in the Bronx. A Crips member spotted him walking home from work one night, snuck up from behind, and put a nine-millimeter slug through the back of his head. Next came Cuddy's uncle, Gerald, whom a Crips enforcer killed at a backyard birthday cookout in Far Rockaway, blowing him away with a revolver before a crowd of shocked partygoers.

A few weeks later, the gang went after Cuddy's 17-year-old niece, Christina. They kidnapped her outside her boyfriend's apartment in Hempstead, Long Island, then drove her to a wooded area, where she was repeatedly gang raped over the course of several hours. Afterward, the Crips left her nude and bloodied, but alive, on Cuddy's stoop—a blue "C," for Crips, scrawled in marker on her back.

Cuddy, when he found her, vowed to kill the four Crips who'd played a role in the rape and murders. He assembled a team of Bloods enforcers, then spent the next few months hunting down and killing or wounding each offending gangster. He compared his crew's mission to that of the Jewish assassins in the film *Munich*, who spent years pursuing terrorists responsible for the murder of 11 Israeli athletes at the 1972 Olympic Games.

His task complete, Cuddy knew he couldn't return to New York; he had seen too much death, had a hand in too many killings, to go back to his old life. It was time to start somewhere new, he felt, before he ended up on the wrong side of a bullet. So Cuddy moved to Baltimore, where his uncle Jerome put him up in a spare bedroom on the city's West Side. And that's where the former Bloods lieutenant was living when I called him in 2013, hoping to interview him for a book I was working on about a long-running Bloods–Crips gang war on Long Island.

"What the hell you calling me for?" he asked, furious that a reporter had gotten hold of his cell phone number.

"Your boys say you're the expert, they have a lot of respect for you," I told him. "I'm just trying to get the story right."

Cuddy's fellow gang members had assured me he knew everything there was to know about the Bloods-Crips conflict—not just on Long Island, but across the country. I asked Cuddy if I could come to Baltimore and interview him. He declined, but we struck up a correspondence, and when my book, *The Triangle: A Year on the Ground with New York's Bloods and Crips*, came out in 2014, Cuddy sent me a text: "You told it fair. You're welcome at my crib anytime."

I took him up on his offer, driving to Baltimore in the hopes of profiling the retired gang lieutenant for *Newsday*, where I cover criminal justice. Cuddy agreed to share his story—the one chronicled here—but didn't want it published at the time, fearing it might reignite his feud with the Crips. Still, we kept in touch, Cuddy making several visits to New York and I to Baltimore. We discussed the possibility of cowriting his autobiography, and were still entertaining the idea when rioting broke out on April 27, 2015.

Seeing Cuddy's text message about the unrest, I jumped on I-95 and drove south as fast as I could. When I arrived, Baltimore was immersed in lawlessness: looters smashing store windows, hurling objects at police, setting vehicles and buildings ablaze. I saw Bloods and Crips members trying to diffuse the violence, standing guard outside businesses to ward off would-be looters. But just as many gang members were partaking in the mayhem, destroying cars, hurling projectiles at police, and threatening to kill cops in retaliation for Freddie Gray's death.

I made plans to meet Cuddy on a West Side corner, and spotted him amid the chaos.

"Glad you came," he said, jumping in my car as we peeled away from a group of rioters, "'cause there's some shit going down people need to know about."

He said our first stop would be the Gilmor Homes—the housing project where Freddie Gray lived before his fatal encounter with police. On the way there, Cuddy told me a remarkable story: Two tech-savvy, 18-year-old project residents, known only by their street names, Brick and Wax, had masterminded a plan to loot dozens of pharmacies, drug corners, and stash houses during the riots. The teens, he said, were in league with Baltimore's Black Guerrilla Family, the city's largest, most powerful gang. Together, they were calling their syndicate Pill City, and they planned to sell their stolen drugs in some of America's poorest neighborhoods.

"BGF out there stealing all kinds of pills, grabbing up whatever they can," Cuddy explained. "And they ain't taking them into white neighborhoods, neither."

Cuddy had learned of the syndicate's plans hours earlier, when a BGF member named Rory Nassim barged into Cuddy's uncle's rowhome, mistaking it for a stash house belonging to Baltimore's longest-serving syndicate boss, Jimmy Masters.

Jimmy's place was actually across the street, a fact Cuddy explained while staring down the barrel of Rory's .38 Special. The New York gangster's reputation preceded him, and when

Rory realized whose home he'd rushed into, he pleaded for forgiveness. As a way to make amends, he offered Cuddy a stake in BGF's looting scheme.

"We about to make a few mill off this craziness," Rory said.

Never one to reject a business proposal outright, Cuddy asked for details. Then he reached out to some of his underworld contacts in Baltimore, several of whom confirmed Rory's story. Pill City really *was* looting scores of drugs across the city and targeting Jimmy Masters's stash spots. The tech-driven syndicate apparently sought to dominate the market for illicit opiates—not just in Baltimore, but across America. "So, you want the story?" Cuddy said as we raced toward Gilmor.

"Of course I want it. It's the craziest thing I've ever heard."

"Yeah, but that's not why I'm giving it to you."

Cuddy explained his motive: Opiates had ravaged his own family, leaving his mother dead of a methadone overdose when he was 16. His stepfather met the same fate seven months later from injecting too much heroin. And while several of Cuddy's relatives had been slain by rival gangsters over the years, many more lost their lives to heroin and pain pills—about 13 family members in all.

"I want this shit to stop," he said later as we walked through Gilmor, Cuddy carrying a Glock 9 millimeter in his waistband in case we ran into trouble. "I don't want to see any more death from that poison, especially among my own people."

I asked Cuddy whether he planned to tell police about the drug looters.

"I can't snitch to no Five-O," he said. "But talking to you, it's a different story. I'm just helping you write about what's going down out here. Way I see it, that's a public service."

I thanked Cuddy and started digging.

That night he pointed out a few locations he'd heard the syndicate was utilizing: BGF safe houses, hangouts, stash spots, and the building in Gilmor where Brick and Wax were thought to reside. He told me everything he knew about the teens, including a supposed email address for them he'd procured from an underworld associate.

"These two boys, people say they're real careful, secretive like," said Cuddy. "Everything they do is on computers."

Afterward, he introduced me to some local gang members participating in the riots. I wrote a story about them for *Newsweek* and continued reporting on the pharmacy lootings.

My first three emails to Brick and Wax went unanswered, but a fourth, sent over an encrypted network, received this response: "Encrypt everything. Always. We want to be anonymous."

I spent the next few weeks learning everything I could about digital encryption, attending crypto parties—online forums where web security experts share tricks of the trade—and reading books about hacking and programming. I wrote a number of stories for *Newsday* about Dark Web drug markets like Silk Road while cultivating relationships with several high-level law enforcement officials—men and women who would later provide crucial guidance for this book.

Then I sent another encrypted email to Brick and Wax.

"I'm taking every precaution," I wrote. "Can we talk?"

In response, the partners sent me elaborate instructions on how to communicate with them going forward. BlackBerrys, iPhones, online aliases, code words, encrypted messaging apps, dummy email addresses—all would be utilized to ensure our correspondence stayed private. After that, I communicated with Brick or Wax almost every day, sending them dozens of questions about their operation, most of which they answered in detail. I learned to distinguish each of their writing styles: When Brick responded, the notes were either full of swagger or colorless and curt, depending on his mood. Wax, in contrast, came off as cautious, courteous, and thorough, sounding more like a Silicon Valley coder than a Baltimore drug dealer.

When we met in person for the first time, I was surprised: Brick and Wax looked even younger than their 18 years. Each wore long-sleeve dress shirts tucked into khakis, hardly the attire I'd expected from a pair of drug dealers.

"Not what you thought, huh?" Brick said, shaking my hand.

His grip was strong, and I understood immediately he was the more aggressive of the two—that his baby face belied the same kind of ruthlessness Cuddy once used to rise through the ranks of New York's underworld.

"Just don't make us regret this," he told me.

We met several more times in 2015, the partners sitting for about 15 hours of in-person interviews in all. All of our other communications occurred over email, by phone, or through encrypted messaging services. The partners' motivation for speaking with me was not complicated: They sought notoriety and fame, both wanting their names to "ring out" in Baltimore long after they were gone. The only way they could ensure that outcome, they said, was to talk to a journalist.

"They only write about gangsters who get caught," Brick said. "But we're not going to [get caught]."

As a precondition of our discussions, I agreed to keep Brick's and Wax's legal names, and several other identifying details, out of my published work. Such arrangements are routine in the world of crime journalism, where protecting a source's anonymity could mean the difference between their living and dying.

As for other underworld figures described in these pages—including members of the Masters Organization—Cuddy acted as an intermediary between myself and these sources, arranging numerous phone interviews and meetings. Combined with the accounts of drug investigators and addiction interrupters, the gangsters' stories allowed me to chronicle Pill City's rise from several key perspectives: those of the syndicate members themselves, of their underworld enemies, and of the authorities and activists trying to thwart both.

Such work was not without risks. I received numerous threats of violence and warnings to stop my reporting on Pill City's activities, with one BGF member, Dante "Slim" Robinson, assuring me I'd be "touched" if I didn't abandon this project. Slim eventually went to jail on a murder charge; Cuddy and I kept on working.

In addition to interviewing more than 300 people for *Pill City*, I've drawn on thousands of pages worth of court filings, medical records, police reports, autopsy records, public health data, Pill City financial records, and other documents. My analysis of these records served as the basis for a number of key statistics in this book and provided important details about hundreds of homicides and overdoses. Because there is often a lag in the release of finalized fatal overdose data by federal, state, and local governments—and some opiate overdoses are not officially counted because of non-standardized reporting procedures and a lack of postmortem testing—I have relied heavily on my own research to gather recent overdose statistics. For data from 2014 and earlier, I've relied heavily on the CDC's WONDER system, which disseminates public health information.

During my reporting for this book, several characters were killed in acts of gun violence, including Brick, Marvin Grier, and Jimmy and Zeke Masters. Other characters are still in the game, incarcerated, or on the run. Pill City is no longer in business, and officially, neither the DEA nor the U.S. Attorney's Office in Baltimore has publicly said how gang members distributed looted drugs after the riots. Their investigation remains active.

But the encrypted syndicate appears to have permanently transformed the drug game in inner-city neighborhoods, bequeathing a lethal legacy to crews like the Youngstown Boys.

"Because of them," Marques says of Pill City, "we're living in a very different environment today than we were in April 2015."

Anyone with an encrypted messaging app and a reliable drug connection can start a business like Brick and Wax did, Marques says. In recent months, copycat crews have cropped up in Chicago, Milwaukee, and St. Louis, using the same business model and encryption technology as Pill City and Youngstown. The trend is also apparent down South, where drug gangs in Atlanta, New Orleans, and South Florida are believed to be running lucrative opiate-dealing operations using nothing but handguns and encrypted messaging software: apps like Adium, Silent Phone, WhatsApp, Apple iMessage, and Wickr. Some crews are even selling product on the Dark Web.

"From on-demand delivery to the use of encryption to inoculate street dealers, these guys [Pill City] didn't just change the way addicts get their drugs—they changed the way people expect to get them, too," Frank Calvacca, the Chicago narcotics detective, told me recently. "And because their tactics are being copied, I don't think that suffering in these neighborhoods . . . is going to end anytime soon."

As for the surviving addicts who figure in this story—

people like Keisha Jones, Leon Marion, and Derek Curry—all are still in recovery. Keisha recently finished a rehab program and filed an appeal to regain custody of her son, Moises. Leon is still working to heal from his car accident, undergoing intensive physical therapy. He was finally able to walk under his own power in January 2016.

As for Curry, he's been clean since February and recently purchased a new guitar.

"It feels good to be playing again and . . . I think Cassie would have liked to see me do it," the musician says. "What I've learned is, life's too short for what ifs. You've just got to go forward, to keep on trying.

"That's what we do in Baltimore," he adds. "We never give up."

—Kevin Deutsch, March 2016, West Baltimore

Acknowledgments

I wish to thank all of the courageous people who helped me report this book. In difficult, often dangerous circumstances, dozens of men, women, and teenagers risked their safety—and sometimes their lives—to help me get the information I needed. Their motive was pure—a desire to save the lives of impoverished Americans not just in Baltimore but across the country. For their assistance, I am forever grateful.

I also wish to thank my mother, Rita Deutsch; my grandmother, Bernice Shulman; my aunt, Lori Shulman; my girlfriend, Elana Joszef; my friend and "fixer" Clarence "Cuddy" Moss; and my colleagues at *Newsday*. Your enthusiasm and support for this project were invaluable, I am forever in your debt.

Thank you to my agent, Jill Marsal; my editor at St. Martin's Press, Emily Carleton; her editorial assistant, Annabella

Hochschild; the attorney who worked on the manuscript, Heather Florence; and the production editor, Donna Cherry.

Thank you to fellow journalists Matthew Chayes, Michael LaForgia, Joe Marino, and Thomas Maier, for inspiring me.

Thank you to my friend Leo Hernandez, who helped spark my love of reading.

Thank you to Stephen Yang and C. S. Muncy for their powerful photographs.

Thank you to the staff of *The Baltimore Sun*, whose reporting on the Freddie Gray riots and ensuing violence proved an invaluable resource for this project.

Thank you to my colleagues at Queens College, especially Gerry Solomon, whose wisdom, advice, and assistance have been invaluable.

Finally, I wish to thank the good people of Baltimore for treating me with such warmth and generosity. You made me feel like I belonged, even in the most trying moments.

Sources

Among others, I've drawn on the following sources during my research:

American Society of Addiction Medicine. "Opioid Addiction 2016 Facts & Figures." http://www.asam.org/docs/default-source/advocacy/opioid-addiction-disease-facts-figures.pdf

American Society of Interventional Pain Physicians. "The American Society of Interventional Pain Physicians (ASIPP) Fact Sheet." October 11, 2011. https://www.asipp.org/documents/ASIPPFactSheet101111.pdf

Baltimore City Criminal Justice Coordinating Council. "Baltimore City Gang Violence Reduction Plan." November 15, 2006. http://www.jhsph.edu/research/centers-and-institutes/center-for-prevention-of-youth-violence/_pdfs/FINALGANGSTRATEGY.pdf

Balzac epigraph in *The Godfather*: https://books.google.com/books?id=CeBLLSBS87sC&pg=PA152&dq=Behind+every+great+fortune+balzac+godfather+epigraph&hl=en&sa=X&ved=0ahUKEwiZ6vSdgpbLAhVHXh4KHeVrAIAQ6AEIJTAA#v=onepage&q=Behind%20

every%20great%20fortune%20balzac%20godfather%20epigraph&f
=false

Bartlett, Jamie. *The Dark Net: Inside the Digital Underworld* (New York: Melville House, 2014).

Baruch College, NYCdata. "World Cities, Top 100 Metropolitan Areas-Ranked by Population, 2014 Estimates." http://www.baruch.cuny.edu /nycdata/world_cities/largest_cities-usa.htm

Bernstein, Lenny, and Higham, Scott. "Investigation: The DEA Slowed Enforcement While the Opioid Epidemic Grew Out of Control." *The Washington Post*, October 22, 2016. https://www.washingtonpost.com /investigations/the-dea-slowed-enforcement-while-the-opioid -epidemic-grew-out-of-control/2016/10/22/aea2bf8e-7f71-11e6 -8d13-d7c704ef9fd9_story.html

Bowman, Lee, and Thomas Hargrove. "Autopsies Reveal Vital Information; Disparities Investigated." *Standard-Times*, August 5, 2009. http://www.gosanangelo.com/news/autopsies-reveal-vital -information-disparities-investigated-ep-441859006-357613901 .html

Broadwater, Luke. "Baltimore Police Acknowledge Mistakes in Freddie Gray's Death." *The Baltimore Sun*, April 24, 2015. http://www.balti moresun.com/news/maryland/bs-md-freddie-gray-protest-prepare -20150424-story.html

Broadwater, Luke, and Yvonne Wegner. "Gov. Hogan Announces $700M Plan to Target Urban Decay in Baltimore." *The Baltimore Sun*, January 5, 2016. http://www.baltimoresun.com/news/maryland/politics /bs-md-ci-hogan-demolition-20160105-story.html#

Bush, George H. W. "Address to the Nation on the National Drug Control Strategy," September 5, 1989. http://www.presidency.ucsb.edu /ws/?pid=17472

Campbell, Colin. "Man Injured in Gilmor Homes Arrest Has Spine Surgery, Remains in Coma." *The Baltimore Sun*, April 15, 2015. http:// www.baltimoresun.com/news/maryland/crime/bs-md-ci-gilmor -homes-arrest-folo-20150415-story.html

Centers for Disease Control and Prevention. "Deaths from Prescription Opioid Overdose." http://www.cdc.gov/drugoverdose/data/overdose .html

———. "Drug Poisoning Mortality: United States, 2002–2014." National Center for Health Statistics, 2016. http://www.cdc.gov/nchs/deaths .htm

———. "Increases in Drug and Opioid Overdose Deaths—United States, 2000–2014." *Morbidity and Mortality Weekly Report (MMWR)*, January 1, 2016. http://www.cdc.gov/mmwr/preview/mmwrhtml/mm 6450a3.htm

———. "Vital Signs: Opioid Painkiller Prescribing." *CDC Vitalsigns*, July 2014. http://www.cdc.gov/vitalsigns/opioid-prescribing/

———. "QuickStats: Number of Deaths from Poisoning, Drug Poisoning, and Drug Poisoning Involving Opioid Analgesics—United States, 1999–2010." *Morbidity and Mortality Weekly Report (MMWR)*, March 29, 2013. http://www.cdc.gov/mmwr/preview/mmwrhtml/mm6212a7.htm

———. "CDC Grand Rounds: Prescription Drug Overdoses—a U.S. Epidemic." *Morbidity and Mortality Weekly Report (MMWR)*, January 13, 2012. http://www.cdc.gov/mmwr/preview/mmwrhtml/mm6101a3.htm

Chayes, Matthew. "'Interrupters' Program Uses Former Gang Members to Combat Street Violence." *Newsday*, August 13, 2014. http://www.newsday.com/news/new-york/interrupters-program-uses-former-gang-members-to-combat-street-violence-1.9053388

Childress, Sarah. "How the Heroin Epidemic Differs in Communities of Color." *Frontline*, February 23, 2016. http://www.pbs.org/wgbh/frontline/article/how-the-heroin-epidemic-differs-in-communities-of-color/

———. "Part II: How the Heroin Epidemic Differs in Communities of Color." *Frontline*, February 23, 2016. http://www.pbs.org/wgbh/frontline/article/how-the-heroin-epidemic-differs-in-communities-of-color/

———. "Part III: How the Heroin Epidemic Differs in Communities of Color." *Frontline*, February 23, 2016. http://www.pbs.org/wgbh/frontline/article/how-the-heroin-epidemic-differs-in-communities-of-color/

Cohen, Andrew. "How White Users Made Heroin a Public-Health Problem." *The Atlantic*, August 12, 2015. http://www.theatlantic.com/politics/archive/2015/08/crack-heroin-and-race/401015/

Cohn, Meredith. "More Drugs Looted from Baltimore Pharmacies Last Year than Previously Reported." *The Baltimore Sun*, August 17, 2016. http://www.baltimoresun.com/bs-hs-looting-drugs-20160817-story.html

Comey, James B. "Going Dark: Are Technology, Privacy, and Public Safety on a Collision Course?" Brookings Institution, October 16, 2014. https://www.fbi.gov/news/speeches/going-dark-are-technology-privacy-and-public-safety-on-a-collision-course

Compton, Wilson M., Christopher M. Jones, and Grant T. Baldwin. "Relationship between Nonmedical Prescription-Opioid Use and Heroin Use." *The New England Journal of Medicine*, January 14, 2016. http://www.nejm.org/doi/full/10.1056/NEJMra1508490?af=R&rss=currentIssue&

DEA Strategic Intelligence Section. *National Herion Threat Assessment Summary* (DEA, June 2016). https://www.dea.gov/divisions/hq/2016/hq062716_attach.pdf

Default. "We Don't Know What's Really Killing Us," *The Davis Enterprise*, September 24, 2009. http://www.davisenterprise.com/Archived-Stories-0/we-don-t-know-what-s-really-killing-us/

Department of Justice, U.S. Attorney's Office, District of Maryland. Press release, "Man Admits to Arson, Looting, Assault and Other Mayhem During Baltimore Riots and Shooting Woman over a $20 Drug Dispute Ten Weeks Later." March 18, 2016. https://www.justice.gov/usao-md/pr/man-admits-arson-looting-assault-and-other-mayhem-during-baltimore-riots-and-shooting

Deutsch, Kevin. "Ross Ulbricht, Founder of Online Drug Site Silk Road, Gets Life in Prison." *Newsday*, May 29, 2015. http://www.newsday.com/news/new-york/ross-ulbricht-founder-of-online-drug-site-silk-road-gets-life-in-prison-1.10488191

———. "Freddie Gray Protests Unite Baltimore Gang Members." *Newsweek*, April 28, 2015. http://www.newsweek.com/freddie-gray-protests-unite-baltimore-gang-members-326503

———. "Long Island's Fentanyl-Related Deaths Peak with Painkiller-Laced Heroin Use." *Newsday*, April 25, 2015. http://www.newsday.com/long-island/long-island-s-fentanyl-related-deaths-peak-with-painkiller-laced-heroin-use-1.10330504

Donelan, Jennifer, and Dwayne Myers. "Heroin Highway: Part 1: 'Baltimore,' Let's Start at the Beginning." ABC7, WJLA, February 15, 2016. http://wjla.com/features/hooked-on-heroin/heroin-highway-part-1-baltimore-lets-start-at-the-beginning

Dwyer, Jim. *More Awesome than Money* (New York: Viking, 2014).

Eban, Katherin. "OxyContin: Purdue Pharma's Painful Medicine." *Fortune*, November 9, 2011, http://fortune.com/2011/11/09/oxycontin-purdue-pharmas-painful-medicine/

Edwards, Jim. "Yes, Bayer Promoted Heroin for Children—Here Are the Ads that Prove It." *Business Insider*, November 17, 2011. http://www.businessinsider.com/yes-bayer-promoted-heroin-for-children-here-are-the-ads-that-prove-it-2011-11

Ellperin, Juliet. "To Battle Opioid Addiction, the Federal Health Department Opens Medication Treatment to More Patients." *The Washington Post*, July 6, 2016. http://www.washingtonpost.com/news/powerpost/wp/2016/07/06/to-battle-opiod-addiction-hhs-opens-medication-treatment-to-more-patients/

Fenton, Justin. "Autopsy of Freddie Gray Shows 'High-Energy' Impact." *The Baltimore Sun*, June 24, 2015. http://www.baltimoresun.com

/news/maryland/freddie-gray/bs-md-ci-freddie-gray-autopsy
-20150623-story.html

Fenton, Justin, and Erica L. Green. "Baltimore Rioting Kicked off with
Rumors of 'Purge.'" *The Baltimore Sun*, April 27, 2015. http://www
.baltimoresun.com/news/maryland/freddie-gray/bs-md-ci-freddie
-gray-violence-chronology-20150427-story.html

Finkel, Ed. "Insurance Coverage for Substance Abuse Improving But Still
Limited." *Juvenile Justice Information Exchange*, July 15, 2015. http://
jjie.org/insurance-coverage-for-substance-abuse-improving-but
-still-limited/116596

Ford, Dana. "Was Freddie Gray's Knife Legal?" *CNN*, May 6, 2015. http://
www.cnn.com/2015/05/06/us/freddie-gray-knife/

Glasser, Gabrielle. "For Mark Willenbring, Substance Abuse Treatment
Begins with Research." *The New York Times*, February 22, 2016.
http://www.nytimes.com/2016/02/23/science/mark-willenbring
-addiction-substance-abuse-treatment.html

Gorman, Anna. "Barriers Remain Despite Health Law's Push to Expand Access to Substance Abuse Treatment." *Kaiser Health News*, April 10, 2014.
http://khn.org/news/substance-abuse-treatment-access-health-law/

Gounder, Celine. "Who Is Responsible for the Pain-Pill Epidemic." *The
New Yorker*, November 8, 2013. http://www.newyorker.com/business
/currency/who-is-responsible-for-the-pain-pill-epidemic

Grassley, Chuck. "Grassley Statement at a Judiciary Committee Hearing
on Opioid Abuse." January 27, 2016. http://www.grassley.senate.gov
/news/news-releases/grassley-statement-judiciary-committee
-hearing-opioid-abuse

Guyuun, Jessica, and Elizabeth Weise. "Lack of Diversity Could Under-
cut Silicon Valley." *USA Today*, August 15, 2014. http://www.usatoday
.com/story/tech/2014/06/26/silicon-valley-tech-diversity-white
-asian-black-hispanic-google-facebook-yahoo/11372421/

Hoyert, D. "The Autopsy, Medicine, and Mortality Statistics." National
Center for Health Statistics, *Vital Health Statistics* 3, no. 32 (2001).
http://www.cdc.gov/nchs/data/series/sr_03/sr03_032.pdf

Jedra, Christina. "Forty-four Charged in Baltimore Jail Scandal; Here's
How the Cases Ended." *The Baltimore Sun*, July 11, 2015. http://www
.baltimoresun.com/news/maryland/sun-investigates/bs-md-sun
-investigates-jail-20150711-story.html

Kamp, Jon, and Arian Campo-Flores. "Parents' Drug Abuse Strains Child-
Welfare Agencies: Growing Epidemic Puts More Children into Foster Care." *The Wall Street Journal*, January 12, 2016. http://www.wsj
.com/articles/parents-drug-abuse-strains-child-welfare-agencies
-1452538476

Lipari, Rachel N., and Arthur Hughes. "Trends in Heroin Use in the United States: 2002 to 2013." National Survey on Drug Use and Health, SAMHSA, *CBHSQ Report*, April 23, 2015. http://www.samhsa.gov /data/sites/default/files/report_1943/ShortReport-1943.html

Mariani, Mike. "Why So Many White American Men Are Dying." *Newsweek*, December 23, 2015. http://www.newsweek.com/2016/01/08 /big-pharma-heroin-white-american-mortality-rates-408354.html ?fb_comment_id=1137272009636618_1137775212919631#f2426f527

———. "How the American Opiate Epidemic Was Started by One Pharmaceutical Company." *The Week*, March 4, 2015. http://theweek.com /articles/541564/how-american-opiate-epidemic-started-by -pharmaceutical-company

Maryland Department of Health and Mental Hygiene. "Drug-and Alcohol-Related Intoxication Deaths in Maryland, 2014." May 2015. http:// dhmh.maryland.gov/data/Documents/Annual%20OD%20 Report%202014_merged%20file%20final.pdf

Meier, Barry. "Tightening the Lid on Pain Prescriptions." *The New York Times*, April 8, 2012. http://www.nytimes.com/2012/04/09/health /opioid-painkiller-prescriptions-pose-danger-without-oversight.html

———. "In Guilty Plea, OxyContin Maker to Pay $600 Million." *The New York Times*, May 10, 2007. http://www.nytimes.com/2007/05/10 /business/11drug-web.htm

Moore, Wes. *The Other Wes Moore: One Name, Two Fates* (New York: Spiegel & Grau, 2011).

Munro, Dan. "Inside the $35 Billion Addiction Treatment Industry." *Forbes*, April 27, 2015. http://www.forbes.com/sites/danmunro/2015 /04/27/inside-the-35-billion-addiction-treatment-industry /#815ff6067fd8

National Institute on Drug Abuse. "Addiction Is a Chronic Disease." http://archives.drugabuse.gov/about/welcome/aboutdrugabuse /chronicdisease/

Oppel Jr., Richard A. "West Baltimore's Police Presence Drops, and Murders Soar." *The New York Times*, June 12, 2015. http://www.nytimes .com/2015/06/13/us/after-freddie-gray-death-west-baltimores -police-presence-drops-and-murders-soar.html

Owens, Pamela L., Marguerite L. Barnett, Audrey J. Weiss, Raynard E. Washington, and Richard Kronick. "Hospital Inpatient Utilization Related to Opioid Overuse Among Adults, 1993–2012." H-CUP, Healthcare Cost and Utilization Project, Agency for Healthcare Research and Quality, Statistical Brief 177, August 2014. http://www .hcup-us.ahrq.gov/reports/statbriefs/sb177-Hospitalizations-for -Opioid-Overuse.pdf

Park, Haeyoun, and Josh Katz. "Murder Rates Rose in a Quarter of the

Nation's 100 Largest Cities." *The New York Times*, September 9, 2016. http://www.nytimes.com/interactive/2016/09/08/us/us-murder-rates.html?hp&action=clicks&pgtype=Homepage&clicksource=story-heading&module=photo-spot-region&region=top-news&WT.nav=top-news

Pietila, Antero. *Not in My Neighborhood: How Bigotry Shaped a Great American City* (Chicago: Ivan R. Dee, 2010).

"Prescription Drugs: OxyContin Abuse and Diversion and Efforts to Address the Problem." GAO Report Number GAO-04-110, December 2003. http://www.gao.gov/htext/d04110.html

Puente, Mark. "Baltimore Records Deadliest Month in More than 40 Years." *The Baltimore Sun*, May 31, 2015. http://www.baltimoresun.com/news/maryland/crime/bs-md-ci-shootings-20150531-story.html

Quinones, Sam. *Dreamland: The True Tale of America's Opiate Epidemic* (New York: Bloomsbury Press, 2015).

Rentz, Catherine. "Video Spotlights Freddie Gray at Baker and Mount Streets." *The Baltimore Sun*, May 20, 2015. http://www.baltimoresun.com/news/maryland/sun-investigates/bs-md-mount-baker-streets-20150520-story.html

Robinson, Lisa. "DEA: Gangs Targeted Pharmacies to Loot During Riots." WBAL TV11, May 28, 2015. http://www.wbaltv.com/news/dea-gangs-targeted-pharmacies-to-loot-during-riots/33269150

———. "'Significant' Arrest Made in Baltimore DEA Raids." WBAL TV11, May 22, 2015. http://www.wbaltv.com/news/significant-arrest-made-in-baltimore-dea-raids/33174498

Rosenberg, Tina. "Part I of II: Medicines to Keep Addiction Away." *The New York Times*, February 16, 2016. http://opinionator.blogs.nytimes.com/2016/02/16/medicines-to-keep-addiction-away/?mtrref=www.google.com&assetType=opinion

———. "Part II of II: Medicines to Keep Addiction Away." *The New York Times*, February 16, 2016. http://opinionator.blogs.nytimes.com/2016/02/16/medicines-to-keep-addiction-away/

Rudd, Rose A., Noah Aleshire, Jon E. Zibbell, and R. Matthew Gladden. "Increases in Drug and Opioid Overdoes Deaths—United States, 2000–2014." CDC Morbidity and Mortality Weekly Report, January 1, 2016. http://www.cdc.gov/mmwr/preview/mmwrhtml/mm6450a3.htm

Schlam, Myles B. "A Law Without Teeth: The Reality of Insurance for Addiction Treatment." *Addiction Treatment Methods, Behavioral Health, Drug Law and Policy, Living with Addiction*, February 12, 2015. http://www.rehabs.com/pro-talk-articles/a-law-without-teeth-the-reality-of-addiction-insurance/

Seelye, Katharine Q. "In Heroin Crisis, White Families Seek Gentler War on Drugs." *The New York Times*, October 30, 2015. http://www.nytimes.com/2015/10/31/us/heroin-war-on-drugs-parents.html?_r=0

Sherman, Natalie. "Count of Businesses Damaged in Riots Rises to About 400." *The Baltimore Sun*, July 23, 2015. http://www.baltimoresun.com/business/bs-bz-business-recovery-20150723-story.html

Steinhauer, Jennifer. "Senate Passes Broad Bill to Combat Drug Abuse." *The New York Times*, March 10, 2016. http://www.nytimes.com/2016/03/11/us/politics/senate-drug-abuse-bill.html

Szabo, Liz. "FDA Approves OxyContin for Kids 11 to 16." *USA Today*, August 14, 2015. http://www.usatoday.com/story/news/2015/08/14/fda-approves-oxycontin-kids/31711929/

Tamayo-Sarver, Joshua H., Susan W. Hinze, Rita K. Cydulka, and David W. Baker. "Racial and Ethnic Disparities in Emergency Department Analgesic Prescriptions." *American Journal of Public Health* 93, no. 12 (December 2003): 2067–2073. http://www.ncbi.nlm.nih.gov/pmc/articles/PMC1448154/

Temple, John. *American Pain: How a Young Felon and His Ring of Doctors Unleashed America's Deadliest Drug Epidemic* (Guilford, CT: Lyons Press, 2015).

———. "DEA Secretly OKs Killer Quantities of Oxy and Morphine." *The Daily Beast*, October 21, 2015. http://www.thedailybeast.com/articles/2015/10/21/dea-secretly-oks-killer-quantities-of-oxy-and-morphine.html

U.S. Department of Health and Human Services. "Facing Addiction in America: The Surgeon General's Report on Alcohol, Drugs, and Health." November 17, 2016. https://addiction.surgeongeneral.gov/surgeon-generals-report.pdf

United States Census Bureau. QuickFacts, Baltimore City, Maryland (County). http://www.census.gov/quickfacts/table/PST045215/24510

van Zee, Art. "The Promotion and Marketing of OxyContin: Commercial Triumph, Public Health Tragedy." *American Journal of Public Health* 99, no. 2 (February 2009): 221–227. http://www.ncbi.nlm.nih.gov/pmc/articles/PMC2622774/

Watkins, D. *The Beast Side: Living (and Dying) While Black in America* (New York: Hot Books, 2015).

Wenger, Yvonne. "Freddie Gray's Twin Sister: 'Please Stop the Violence.'" *The Baltimore Sun*, April 26, 2015. http://www.baltimoresun.com/news/maryland/baltimore-city/bs-md-ci-freddie-gray-sister-20150426-story.html

Win, Leana. Testimony on America's Heroin and Opioid Abuse Epidemic. March 22, 2016. https://oversight.house.gov/wp-content/uploads/2016/03/Wen-Baltimore-Statement-3-22-Heroin-Opioid-Abuse.pdf

Leabharlanna Poiblí Chathair Bhaile Átha Cliath
Dublin City Public Libraries

extracts reading groups
competitions books new
discounts extracts
extracts
reading groups
competitions
discounts events
books
new
reading groups
events
books
extracts
new books
title
extracts
new reading groups
interviews
events extracts extracts
discounts
events
new books events
books
events
interviews new books extracts
events new

discounts extracts discounts

www.panmacmillan.com

extracts events reading groups
competitions books extracts new
books